LIV CHINA

Other How To Books on Living & Working Abroad

Applying for a United States Visa
Become an Au Pair
Do Voluntary Work Abroad
Emigrate
Find a Job in Canada
Finding Work Overseas
Find Temporary Work Abroad
Get a Job Abroad
Get a Job in America
Get a Job in Australia
Get a Job in Europe
Get a Job in France
Get a Job in Germany
Get a Job in Hotels & Catering
Get a Job in Travel & Tourism
Live & Work in America
Live & Work in Australia
Live & Work in France
Live & Work in Germany
Live & Work in the Gulf
Live & Work in Hong Kong
Live & Work in Italy
Live & Work in Japan
Live & Work in New Zealand
Live & Work in Portugal
Live & Work in Saudia Arabia
Live & Work in Spain
Living & Working in Britain
Living & Working in Canada
Living & Working in China
Living & Working in the Netherlands
Master Languages
Obtaining Visas & Work Permits
Rend & Buy Property in France
Rent & Buy Property in Italy
Retire Abroad
Selling into Japan
Setting Up Home in Florida
Spend a Year Abroad
Study Abroad
Teach Abroad
Travel Round the World
Working Abroad
Working as a Holiday Rep
Working in Japan
Working in the Gulf
Working on Contract Worldwide
Working on Cruise Ships
Your Own Business in Europe

Other titles in preparation

The How To series now contains more than 150 titles in the following categories:

Business Basics
Family Reference
Jobs & Careers
Living & Working Abroad
Student Handbooks
Successful Writing

Please send for a free copy of the latest catalogue for full details (see back cover for address).

How To Books

LIVING & WORKING ABROAD

LIVING & WORKING IN CHINA

How to obtain entry and plan a successful stay

Christine Hall

How To Books

Other books by the same author

How to Get a Job in Germany
How to Live and Work in Germany
How to be a Freelance Journalist
How to Work in Retail (with Sylvia Lichfield)
Living and Working in Britain

British Library Cataloguing-in-Publication data
A catalogue record for this book is available from the British Library.

First published in 1996 by How To Books Ltd, Plymbridge House, Estover Road, Plymouth PL6 7PZ, United Kingdom.

Note: The material contained in this book is set out in good faith for general guidance and no liability can be accepted for loss or expense incurred as a result of relying in particular circumstances on statements made in the book. The laws and regulations are complex and liable to change, and readers should check the current position with the relevant authorities before making personal arrangements.

Produced for How To Books by Deer Park Productions.
Typeset by Kestrel Data, Exeter.
Printed and bound in Great Britain by
Cromwell Press, Broughton Gifford, Melksham, Wiltshire.

Contents

List of Illustrations

Preface

Just over two years ago, I accepted a job in China. I was to be copy editor of an educational newspaper in English language, in a town called Tonghua somewhere near the North Korean Border.

Three months remained between decision and departure, and I was desperate to get as much information as possible. My list of questions was enormous.

What did I need to pack, and what should I leave at home? Can you buy a hairdryer in the Jilin Province? Should I take a tape recorder or a shortwave radio? What about tampons, cosmetics, medicines? Typewritter ribbons? Will there be shoes available, large enough for western feet?

Should I start learning Mandarin Chinese, or wait until I'm in the country? Will parcels from Britain arrive? Will I be lonely so far away from all western culture? Can I make friends with the Chinese—aren't they all very reserved? What is the dress code in a Chinese office?

What is the weather like in the Jilin Province? Will I be able to afford travelling on a Chinese salary? Do I need a rabies vaccination? Is it possible to remain vegetarian? What if there is another critical situation like the Tiananmen incident, or even another 'cultural revolution'? Will I be safe?

I asked everyone of my acquaintances who had ever visited China. But although the tourists could advise me on which temples to visit and how much to tip hotel staff, their knowledge of life in China away from the tourist attractions was nil. Those who had lived in China, even as recently as five or ten years ago, admitted that their experiences were no longer relevant.

Library books provided interesting reading. But they focussed on customs and traditions, or gave accounts of travels in China at the turn of the century. Guidebooks graded the quality of hotel rooms, but not the reliability of washing machines.

In China, I met many other westerners who had been in the same situation. They would have wanted a book which helped them prepare their stay in China and also helped survive in a different and often difficult environment.

Problems which take you by surprise—in my case, the erratic water supplies, the lack of hygiene in healthcare—can make your life unpleasant. If you know what difficulties to expect, you'll be prepared and can deal with them easily. The more you know about living in China, a country with culture so rich and so different from ours, the more you can enjoy your stay.

More than fifty people, working in different provinces and in various professions, have contributed their experiences, suggestions and information. I wish to thank them for giving their time and advice so generously: Fiona Ferry, Hendrik Jan Groenenberg, Joyce and Derek Jackson, Heather Dumchen, Mark Prior, Layla Mewburn and the others who wish to remain unnamed.

Others who helped me with the research and deserve thanks include: Laura Rivkin of the Great Britain–China Centre; Jay Lloyd-Smith and Nicholas Maclean-Bristol of the Trust Fund; David Creffield of Overseas Jobs Express; Gina Corrigan of Occidor Travel; Nick Phillips; Lucien Harrington of British Executive Service Overseas, and everyone else for their contributions large and small.

Christine Hall

Acknowledgements

Grateful thanks to all the people in China who gave me their friendship and support while I was in China, who went out of their way to make my stay a happy one, and who helped me with the research for this book: fellow volunteers Sarah Lowis and Phil Horton; all my colleagues at the *English Coaching Paper*, especially editors Ding, Lisa, Joy, Kitty, Wang and Liu, accountant Liang, driver Liu and publisher Bao; Sue Milner and her colleagues at the VSO field office in Beijing; Jan Weaver; Professor Cheng and the staff at the Sino–German Policlinic in Beijing; Zhang Hai Xiang, a middle school teacher who campaigns for better teacher training; my case study interviewees Fiona Ferry, Hendrik Jan Groenenberg, Joyce and Derek Jackson, Heather Dumchen, Mark Prior, Layla Mewburn and the others who wish to remain unnamed; and of course all my Chinese friends at the Teachers' College in Tonghua, who were my friends as well as hosts/interpreters/guides/language teachers/dance teachers, especially Carol, Li (Sally), Cathy, Xiao (Jessica), Heather, Zhin (Connie), Han, Wang, Ruth and Joan.

Many thanks also to everyone else who helped me research and write this book: Laura Rivkin of the Great Britain–China Centre; Jay Lloyd-Smith and Nicholas Maclean-Bristol of the Trust Fund; David Creffield of Overseas Jobs Express; Gina Corrigan of Occidor Travel; Nick Phillips; Lucien Harrington of British Executive Service Overseas; and everyone else for their contributions large and small.

Finally, thanks to fellow writers Claire Gill, Diana Lloyd-Taylor, Mary Victoria Webb, Lynda Rajan, Norman Toulson, Primrose Cummings and Andy Saunders for their advice on, and proofreading of, some of the chapters, and Jung Chang, author of *Wild Swans*, for her kind encouragement for this book.

Making International Phone Calls

The country code you dial before the area code depends not only on where you are phoning to, but also on where you are phoning from. Therefore, all phone numbers in this book are given with the area code, but without the country code.

To make an international phone call, you dial the 'international call' code. From most countries, it is 00. Then you dial the country code. This is usually a two or three digit number.

86	China (People's Republic)
886	China (Taiwan)
44	UK
1	USA

If you cannot get a call through to China, it is probably because the telephone network is hopelessly overloaded. It can take a day to make a local phone call in Beijing. It could also be that the telephone number has changed. Especially in rapidly developing areas, extra digits are added every few months to accommodate the increasing number of new connections.

1
Meeting the Challenge

LOOKING AT CHINA'S HISTORY

Archaeological findings show that China was inhabited by humans as long as five hundred thousand to one million years ago. The first Chinese dynasty, the Xia, was established in the twenty-first century before Christ, which was the beginning of a society whose wealth depended on the work of many slaves.

The years 770 to 221 BC experienced the change from slave to feudal society which lasted until the nineteenth century. The first unified, multi-national state in Chinese history, the Qin dynasty, began in 221 BC.

The dynasty ruled for two thousand years but was overthrown as a result of the Opium War. Foreign traders were importing opium to China on such a large scale that the empire had the serious economic problem how to pay for it—there was not enough silver currency. The Chinese government prohibited opium trade. Britain decided to protect the trade in which it had invested a lot of money. This led to a war which started in 1840 and to victory for the British. China was forced to accept a number of unfavourable treaties with other states.

A democratic revolution, led by Dr Sun Yat-sen, overthrew the government in 1911. But instead of a democratic, egalitarian state free from foreign oppression, it led to a situation where local dictators (warlords) fought each other. The country was weakened and split.

Chiang Kai-shek, leader of the National Party, led an expedition against the warlords, defeated them, and tried to make China a modern, unified nation. But then the National Party (Kuomintang) and the Communist Party (Gongchantang) split, and for two years the country was torn by a civil war.

In addition China suffered from the Japanese invasion which began in 1932.

Under Mao Zedong, the communists achieved victory and on 1 October 1949, the People's Republic of China was declared. The Chinese refer to this as the 'Liberalisation'.

During the first years, the communists accomplished a lot. The land was taken away from the landlords and given to the peasants. However, this system was soon replaced by collectivisation, where everything was owned and organised by communes. After a few years, this led to a drop in productivity.

The government then launched the 'Great Leap Forward', promising a miracle in economic development. Farmers were urged to produce steel in their farmyards. Farm work was neglected which led to a man-made famine in which millions of people starved to death. And the steel produced in this way was of such low quality that much of it was useless.

Mao's next well-meant project was the 'Cultural Revolution', which led to an equal disaster. He called the youth of China in 1966 to wipe out everything old and traditional. The managers of hospitals, railways and factories were sent to do forced labour, often even tortured or killed. The same fate awaited many intellectuals. Knowledge and skills were destroyed with the people who possessed them. A whole generation was deprived of proper schooling.

After Mao's death and the end of the 'Cultural Revolution', China was a weak, poor, powerless nation.

The new plans for China, disclosed by Deng Xiaoping in 1978, allowed farmers to work in small groups and families again, instead of for co-operatives. They could decide what to plant, and sell it in the market. Within five years, agricultural production doubled!

INTRODUCING CHINA TODAY

How do the recent changes towards international trade and a free market affect the average Chinese?

- Profit-making is the best motivation for a peasant family. More food is produced and sold in the markets, which means better supplies with food for all. Both quantity and variety of food supplies have increased.

- The living standard is higher. Many Chinese, especially in the towns and cities, can afford a fridge, a washing machine and a television. These items are considered status symbols, and the fridge is often placed in the centre of the living room for everyone to see and envy.

- Not surprisingly, the profit-making spirit has its dark side. Many Chinese, especially the older people, regret that there is more greed, and less idealism. It appears that the increase of wealth has also led to an increase in corruption.

- Inter-personal relations among members of a family, among neighbours, friends or colleagues are not as good as they used to be. People have become more selfish and competitive.

- For the first time, they have the chance to get in touch with the outside world, to learn what is going on elsewhere. This can be a challenging as well as a confusing experience. During the 'Cultural Revolution', the Chinese were brainwashed to hate all foreigners; now they are encouraged to value them as advisers. The image they have of the west is often one of glitz, glamour, fast cars and unlimited wealth, which is what they see in American video films.

- The Chinese have more confidence in the future. They feel that they can, to some extent, shape their own future, instead of having everything planned and decided for them.

- There are more opportunities to learn new skills.

- Many Chinese fear unemployment and poverty, and the loss of their pensions, because work units no longer provide the secure jobs and pensions to which the Chinese workers have been accustomed.

- While the overall wealth increases, the gaps between rich and poor are widening dramatically.

- Prices rise drastically, the inflation is huge.

Phil, an English teacher in Tonghua (north east China) describes how quickly changes take place: 'When I arrived two years ago, the male students were still wearing dark blue Mao suits. The women were experimenting with muted colours. My students were amazed at my red jumpers! Look at them now. The girls wear bright red and purple clothes, covered in sequins, beads and fringes, and the boys wear western suits with white trainers, or leisure outfits in fluorescent colours. Looking at Tonghua, a quarter of the town's buildings have been torn down and replaced by something bigger and bolder.'

DISCOVERING YOUR OPPORTUNITIES

China is opening towards the west. Foreign trade is encouraged and develops at an astonishing pace. If you browse in High Street shops, looking at shirts, sweaters, bags, rucksacks and accessories, you'll discover the label 'Made in China'.

Everyone in China, it seems, wants to get involved in import, export, tourism, finance or another business sector which offers the chance of quick wealth. For many this dream has become true already, especially in the coastal cities.

But there are limits to the growth, and one of these limits is the lack of marketing, finance and language skills.

For most of its history, the country was closed to the outside world, and most Chinese never came in touch with the outside world. Few Chinese were encouraged to learn foreign languages, and there were times when one could get arrested for talking to a foreigner in the street.

Now that foreign languages and foreign trade are desirable, and promoted by the government, there are not enough people who possess the necessary skills and can teach them.

The Chinese government is eager to close the gap by inviting foreign experts to train Chinese counterparts. Every year, many hundreds of experts and teachers from the USA, the UK, Japan, Canada and other countries follow the call. The number is increasing.

Foreign companies are encouraged to set up joint ventures in China, producing goods suitable for export, and foreign investors are invited to invest in the still volatile but increasingly interesting stock market.

The employment opportunities are considerable, especially for teachers and graduates with training skills, engineers, marketing, foreign trade and finance experts.

Job opportunities exist with Chinese owned businesses and work units, international companies, Sino-foreign joint ventures and Chinese government organisations. Payment is low, if converted into western currency, which can make it difficult to keep up financial commitments (such as a mortgage) at home, but most foreign experts can live comfortably on their earnings in China.

If you get a job with a western employer, at a western payment level, you can live comfortably and put aside considerable savings, because the living costs are low.

TWELVE REASONS TO GO TO CHINA

1. Good job prospects.
2. Low living cost.
3. English is spoken widely, especially in the cities.
4. Chance to experience a different culture.
5. Variety—every part of China is different.
6. It is easy to make friends with the Chinese.
7. You can contribute to China's opening, by introducing new ideas and ways of thinking.
8. Adventure—you can find parts still untouched by western civilisation.
9. You are free to practise your religion (but not to preach it).
10. There are no restrictive dress codes.
11. Women have the same status and opportunities as men (well, almost).
12. China covers several climatic zones, and you are likely to find a place which suits your health.

However, China is not the ideal country for everyone. Bear in mind that your earnings in China may not be enough to keep up financial commitments at home. To live in a foreign country, perhaps in an extremely cold or hot climate, without the medical care you are accustomed to, you must be physically strong and reasonably healthy. You cannot always speak your opinion freely. You may encounter a lot of bureaucracy and even corruption. The Chinese have no concept of privacy, and you may have to cope with frequent intrusions. It can be difficult to obtain appropriate schooling and healthcare for your children.

LOOKING AT THE MAP

How big is China? This is not only a geographical, but also a political question. The answer depends on the viewpoint you take. For example, the official People's Republic of China viewpoint is that Tibet is one of its autonomous regions and that Taiwan is one of its provinces—and not everyone would agree. (See Fig 1.)

According to the China National Tourist Office, China has a total land area of 9.6 million square kilometres. From north to south, it measures some 5,500 kilometres, and from west to east about 5,200 kilometres.

China's land border is 22,800 kilometres long. The mainland coast, 18,000 kilometres long, is dotted with harbours and ports, the most famous of them, from north to south, being Dalian, Qinhuangdao, Tianjin, Yantai, Qingdao, Lianyungang, Nantong, Shanghai, Ningbo, Wenzhou, Fuzhou, Xiamen, Guangzhou, Zhanjiang and Beihai.

Shanghai is the largest city in China with a population of 13.37 million, and the best developed industry, commerce and ocean transportation within China.

Beijing (which used to be known as Peking in the west) is the capital of the People's Republic of China, as well as the country's political, economic and cultural centre. It has a population of 10.82 million, and a history of 800 years as a national capital.

There are three administrative divisions: provinces, autonomous regions, and municipalities directly under the central government. The official Chinese version is that there are twenty-three provinces (the official version counts Taiwan as part of the PR China), five autonomous regions (including Tibet) and three centrally administered municipalities.

China is a multinational country with over fifty ethnic groups (the official PR China version says fifty-six).

According to the 1990 national census, there were 1.4248 billion Han people, accounting for 91.96 per cent of China's total population. The other 55 nationalities represent 91.2 million people, or 8.04 per cent of the total.

The Han nationality has its own spoken and written language,

Map of China

This map is a sketch by the author, to show where the provinces are located. It is not intended as a political statement.

known as the Chinese language (Mandarin) which is commonly used throughout China and is a working language of the United Nations. The Hui and Manchu nationalities also use this language. The other ethnic groups use the spoken languages of their own; 23 minority nationalities have their own written languages.

COPING WITH THE CLIMATE

Most of China is situated in the temperate zone, but parts of south China are located in the tropical and subtropical zones, while the northern part is near the frigid zone.

In north China, summers are warm and short and winters long and cold. In the tropical and subtropical south, trees and other vegetation remain green all year. The southeastern coastal regions of China are warm and humid and have four distinct seasons.

The temperatures in the interior areas of northwest China change greatly during the daytime. There is a saying: 'People wear fur coats in the morning and silk at noon'.

Because of its high elevation, the Quinghai Tibet Plateau area, a special alpine-cold zone, has low temperatures all year round.

If you go to a remote place, it can be difficult to obtain precise information about the weather and the climate there. The area may not be mentioned in guidebooks. Or your employer, desperate to get a foreign teacher, may choose not to mention that the average winter temperature is somewhere around –20 to –30 degrees centigrade. Make an effort to find out! Almost every climate can be endured, but only if you are well prepared.

North of the Yangzi River, most houses, schools, hotels and public buildings have central heating. But south of the river, the concrete buildings are unheated. Unfortunately, the cold does not always stop precisely at the river line. For several days or weeks per year the people in central China (or even in the south) have to cope with freezing temperatures, with no heating available. Wherever you go, take some woollen socks and thermal underwear —see Chapter 3, Getting Ready.

Case studies

Hendrik Jan writes from the Jianxi Province: 'It's subtropical here. This means it's hot and humid during the summer, very wet in June. Right now half the province is flooded, it has been raining for almost a month. Last weekend we had a goodbye party for some colleagues who are leaving. The party was in Jian. About half way to Nanchang we had to sail through a city. Quingjiang had 1 metre water level in the streets.

'The winter is cold. Between zero and ten degrees Centigrade with occasional frost or snow. This may not sound very bad; but in houses without heating it's bloody cold, I can tell you. I've been cursing a lot when my little heater broke down again.

'I was going with Voluntary Service Overseas, and because the VSO information said I was going to a subtropical area I didn't bring enough warm clothing. I really regretted that during the winter time.'

Mark lives in Hohhot (Inner Mongolia): 'The summers are very nice—hot but not roasting. Winters are freezing, but the flats are well heated and double-glazed. Outside you wear a down jacket, locally made sheepskin gloves and several layers of longjohns, then you're OK. The worst bit is that spring is windy and very dusty. Dust gets everywhere, it can't be helped.'

Heather Dumchen reports from Xingyi (Guizhou Province): 'It's warm and wet in the summer, cool and wet in the winter (yuck). I love the warmth, don't mind the wet in the summer, but hate the cold and wet. I arrived in March and caught the end of the cold wet winter weather and didn't like it one bit. April and May are very nice, warm and dry.'

Joyce and Derel are based in Loudi (Hunan Province): 'The climate is quite extreme. It's July now and it is very hot and sticky— and likely to get hotter. We find it very difficult even with an air conditioner in the bedroom, and are dreading August when we are told it becomes an oven.'

POPULATION GROWTH

In 1949, there were 541,670,000 people living on the mainland. Lacking controls and appropriate education on the subject, the population increased to 806,710,000 by 1969.

Faced with the serious problem of feeding the growing population, the government implemented family planning in 1970. Since then, the birth rate has declined each year. The birth rate dropped 34.11 to 19.69 per thousand. The natural growth rate declined from 26.08 to 12.98 per thousand—which is still too high, considering that almost every possible square inch in China is farmed already!

Late marriage and late childbirth are promoted, and couples are permitted only one child. In rural areas, couples may have a second baby, and couples living in a minority area may have more children. Most Chinese accept the system in principle. Potential conflicts arise where the firstborn is a handicapped child, and sometimes even when the child is female. Despite government propaganda, showing healthy families with one happy girl child, many Chinese still long for a male heir.

CARING FOR THE ENVIRONMENT

As in many developing countries, the economic development is at the cost of the environment. Regulations to protect the environment exist, but cannot always be reinforced, and are often not sufficient. Chemicals leak into streams, toxic fumes are discharged into the air. You will see litter wherever you go—whole villages are disfigured by piles of rubbish, and villagers wash their clothes in heavily littered streams.

Your Chinese friends will admit there is a problem, but continue to drop their litter everywhere. 'But we are a developing country,' they say, as if this explained and justified everything.

Don't lose your temper, or show any impatience. The best method of educating your Chinese without anyone losing face is to pick up the litter they leave behind on the picnic quietly, with a smile. They will quickly follow your example.

If you are a teacher, you can include the subject in your lessons, for intensive readings or for discussions. However, make sure you tackle it in a general way, so that you don't appear to be criticising China or the Chinese.

PRACTISING YOUR RELIGION

Today, everyone can practise their religion freely, whether they are Muslims, Buddhists, Christians or members of other religions. For example, if you are a Christian you will be welcome to join the nearest church. There are protestant as well as catholic churches. The only problem could be that services are held in the

Chinese language, and you may not find them valuable to you if you don't understand a word.

However, religious life is strictly regulated and supervised by the state. The government fears that unwelcome, foreign ideas could infiltrate China through international churches. Therefore, the Chinese churches are completely separated from the church organisations in other countries. Very little contact and exchange is permitted.

If you decide to join a church, your activities within the group will be closely monitored. If you start teaching or preaching your faith, or suggest any idea which is done in the church in your home country and should be taken up in China, you make yourself suspect and may be expelled from the country. It is alright to show photos of church services and religious festivals in your country, but otherwise tread carefully.

An organisation which liaises with Chinese churches is: The Council of Churches for Britain and Ireland, China Department, 35–41 Lower Marsh, London SE1 7RL. Tel: (0171) 620 4444. Fax: (0171) 928 0010.

CELEBRATING HOLIDAYS AND FESTIVALS

The following official holidays are celebrated by all Chinese people:

- New Year's Day on 1 January
- Spring Festival (on the first three days of the Chinese lunar year)
- Labour Day on 1 May
- National Day on 1 October

In addition, some areas or population groups celebrate the following:

- Women's Day on 8 March
- Youth Day on 4 May
- Children's Day on 1 June
- Army Day on 1 August
- and various festivals of the minorities

THINKING ABOUT HUMAN RIGHTS

If you decide to go to China, you must be aware that many human rights—by western definition—are violated. Some of your experiences in China may make you feel angry or helpless, depending on your temperament. But you must also be aware that you cannot change things. The Chinese government has invited you as an expert in your trade, not as a political reformer.

By all means, observe what is happening, and how it is affecting the people around you. Feed back your observations, positive and negative, to human rights organisations after your return. But while you are in China, remember that you are a guest of the country, and behave like one.

Protesting loudly against perceived injustice will only lead to you being expelled from the country, which helps nobody. And it may even get your Chinese friends into trouble.

It helps to remember that in the Chinese way of thinking, the well-being of the individual is of less importance than the well-being of the group. From this point of view, it is logical that the individual's human rights have, in certain circumstances, been sacrificed in the interest of the community.

In addition, the Chinese view is that a decent living standard, with basic education and enough food for all, is the most important human right. The government says that this must be achieved first; the other human rights will be addressed later.

Another point to bear in mind is that there is no country in the world, especially not among the developing countries, where violation of human rights does not occur. Even in the 'highly civilised' western world, frightening abuses happen.

But by just being there, by sharing their life and by telling them about life in your home country, by being their window to the outside world, you are contributing to one human right the Chinese were previously denied: the right for information.

TIANANMEN AND ALL THAT

China's attitudes to foreigners have changed rapidly, from one extreme to the other. There is no guarantee that foreigners will not be persecuted again one day. But observers think it is highly unlikely. The Chinese enjoy their newly found wealth too much to deprive themselves of one of its main sources.

But what if a rebellion or civil war breaks out while you are in China?

In 1989 students gathered to demonstrate in Tiananmen Square, calling for political changes to the communist system. A few hooligans among the students attacked soldiers who were under strict orders that under no circumstances should they fire into the crowds. Despite attempts at a peaceful solution, the situation escalated into a violent event which ended by tanks being ordered to roll, crushing demonstrators who stood in the way. For a while, it seemed as if China was on the verge of a civil war.

These events can give an indication of what would happen in a similar situation. Foreigners staying in China at that time were hardly affected by the events. The worst some had to endure was that they were asked to return to their hotels and to stay there for a couple of days. This is reassuring.

However, with a view to China's history, and bearing in mind how unpredictable political situations, rebellions and civil wars can be, it is a good idea to be prepared to leave China at short notice.

Again, looking at Tiananmen Square, international flights were quickly booked out. However, those with foreign currency (especially Sterling or US dollars in cash or travellers cheques) were still able to obtain a seat.

Be prepared for an emergency by:

- Registering with the embassy of your country in Beijing.

- Investigating immediately on arrival at your posting the timetables for trains and buses to Beijing or out of the country.

- Finding out how much a plane ticket from Beijing to your home country (or to Hong Kong) costs, and keeping a sufficient reserve in travellers cheques.

- Keeping enough Chinese cash to buy train tickets (bearing in mind that in an emergency you may have to pay inflated prices or bribes).

TAIWAN OR MAINLAND CHINA?

There are two states, both called China. One is the People's Republic of China, also known as 'communist China' and 'mainland China'.

The other is the Republic of China, which is also called by the name of its main island 'Taiwan' (formerly 'Formosa').

From 1949, when the communists took over the government of mainland China, it became the refuge of the defeated Chinese nationalist government under Chiang Kai-Shek.

Until 1971, the government of Taiwan was regarded by the United Nations as the official government of all China, ignoring the fact that for over twenty years the largest part of China had a different government.

In 1971, the People's Republic of China was recognised as a state by the United Nations, and in consequence, Taiwan was expelled!

The government of the People's Republic of China claims that Taiwan is nothing but a province of its own state, despite Taiwan's independence for over forty years.

In practice, the two countries are usually regarded and treated as separate states with different governments, and many nations are engaged in foreign trade with both.

Many foreigners prefer living in Taiwan to living in mainland China, because it is more 'westernised' and the economy is better developed. This can lessen the 'culture shock' and make it a little easier to adapt to the environment. English teachers sometimes spend a year in Taiwan, learning about Chinese language and culture, before they move on to live in the People's Republic to experience a more 'different' culture.

Note: Unless indicated otherwise, all information contained in this book refers to the People's Republic of China.

FINDING OUT MORE

Spending your holidays in China

If you can afford it, it is a good idea to explore China as a tourist first. This will give you a good impression of the culture, climate, and mentality, and if you are suited to it. Some organisers offer tours 'off the beaten track', which are, for your purpose, preferable to the usual tombs and temples tours. If possible, choose a tour to a province where you are likely to look for employment. Don't go on your own: the difficulty of obtaining a ticket to the next station alone can make your trip fail. Unlike other countries, China is not a country to explore on your own, until you have built a network of connections and know how to get a ticket to your next destination (see Chapter 5 on travel in China).

The following are some tour operators who deal with 'off the beaten track':

- **Occidor** is a tour operator which organises tours which explore, for example, the ethnic minorities, festivals, embroidery/textiles/weaving, Burma Road, the route of the Long March, Chinese brush painting, nature reserves, the route of the silk road, steam railways, etc. Accommodation and travel are sometimes basic because they are outside the usual tourist areas. Contact: Gina Corrigan, Occidor, 10 Broomcroft Road, Bognor Regis, Sussex PO22 7NJ. Tel: (01243) 582178. Fax: (01243) 587239.

- **World Expeditions** organises bike ride tours along small side roads, stopping at small villages, schools, factories and markets. Occasionally, the company organises slide and video presentations in London. Admission to these events is free. In addition, World Expeditions has a China video which can be borrowed for free. Contact: World Expeditions, 7 North Road, Maidenhead SL6 1PE. Tel: (01628) 74174. Fax: (01628) 74312.

- **Cultural Tours Ltd** offers tailor-made tours for groups of specialists, for example justices, horticulturists, architects, farmers, train enthusiasts, church fellowships, doctors, artists, photographers and gourmets. Itineraries always include meetings with top Chinese experts in their particular field of interest. The company also organises custom designed tours for individual travel. Address: 320 Regent Street, London W1R 5AB. Tel: (0171) 636 7906. Fax: (0171) 436 3053.

Further information on travelling to China is available from The China National Tourist Office, 4 Glentworth Street, London

NW1. Tel: (0891) 200273 (you will be charged for your call!) or from your local travel agents.

Reading up on the subject

Cheaper than travelling to China is, of course, buying or borrowing books and videos, or attending lectures.

Culture Shock! China and *Wild Swans* have been recommended by many interviewees. For details of these books and other suggested literature, see the Further Reading section at the end of this book. You can also ask your local librarian for advice. Most lending libraries are able to borrow specific books from other libraries for you, if they don't have them in stock, charging a fee of around 50 pence for the service.

Joining the Great Britain–China Centre

Based in London, the Great Britain–China Centre is an independent organisation which is run by a small committed team of Chinese speakers. It receives an annual grant-in-aid from the Foreign and Commonwealth Office, and raises project funds from the private sector.

The Centre provides reliable information on China and Sino-British relations. The staff have first-hand experience of China and advise companies and individuals in Britain who want to establish contact with China. They also provide pre-departure briefings on political, economic and social developments in China. In addition, they compile and publish the Directory of *British Organisations with a China Interest*, and are currently expanding their contracts across Europe.

The Great Britain–China Centre has a substantial library with over 4,000 English-language books on all aspects of China, a large selection of current newspapers and magazines in English and Chinese, press clippings, slides and videos. Members can borrow books, and postal loans can be arranged.

Among other projects, the Centre organises exchanges of exhibitions, writers, artists and performers. It also finds young Chinese professionals work placements in Britain, to give them on-the-job training and exposure to modern management methods.

Membership is open to individuals and organisations.

Benefits include:

- Monthly lectures on Chinese current affairs, society and culture.
- Seminars, library talks and opportunities to meet members and Chinese visitors on a social basis.
- Regular mailings on forthcoming events countrywide.
- Free copy of British–China, a magazine which is published three times a year and contains articles, reviews and news of Sino–British exchanges and developments in China.
- Use of the library.
- Chinese evening classes.

Membership costs £15 per year, with reductions for students, couples, and those living outside London and the Home Counties. Contact: The Great Britain–China Centre, 15 Belgrave Square, London SW1X 8PS. Tel: (0171) 235 6696. Fax: (0171) 245 6885.

2
Finding a Job

Getting a job in China is not difficult, but you have to know where to look. Be prepared to spend a while job hunting, and to wait for weeks (months) until you get a reply to your request for information, or your application letter is acknowledged. Bureaucracy can slow down the procedure.

WHERE TO FIND THE JOBS

The Chinese government actively invites 'foreign experts' and 'foreign teachers'. Qualified and experienced technicians, experts in international trade and finance, as well as teachers (especially language and music teachers) are much in demand.

Other skills areas also offer vacancies, although in smaller numbers: You have a good chance, for example, as a teacher for western-style hairdressing or as a chef for western cuisine, but you won't be able to choose among many vacancies.

The best paid jobs can be found in the big cities and in the coastal provinces.

A teacher, on the other hand, who doesn't mind a lower salary and living standard, or a colder climate, could go to Inner Mongolia, northeast China, or any remote rural place, and find schools begging them to teach.

Taiwan, too, offers good job prospects, because of a labour shortage. The government motivates women to return to work and have careers, and subsidises daycare centres for children and the elderly to enable more women to join the workforce. Domestic and childcare work is an area wide open to foreigners.

English language teaching also provides excellent opportunities, and most teachers find a job within a week or two. Apparently, there is also demand for westerners modelling for fashion and advertising. These are well-paid temp jobs.

The newspaper *Overseas Jobs Express* and the magazine *Jobs International* sometimes carry situations vacant advertisements by employers or sending agencies, for Mainland China and Taiwan.

If you have no particular qualifications or experience, consider investing in a one-month TEFL course which prepares you for teaching English as a foreign language. The Chinese demand for English teachers is insatiable and is likely to increase over the next few years, both in mainland China and in Taiwan.

GOING WITH A SENDING AGENCY

There are benefits, as well as drawbacks, if you decide to sign on with an agency which posts people to China instead of investigating openings yourself.

Advantages

- Jobs with sending organisations are easier to find and more accessible, because you can apply to an address in your home country. You may even find the jobs advertised in the national press.

- You are likely to find a job faster, and may have a wider choice of jobs.

- Sending organisations have the experience which you (probably) don't have. They know the country, the institutions and the pitfalls. They vet the jobs for you, and can, in short, save you a lot of trouble.

- Because they represent many job applicants, they are in a stronger position than you as an individual to negotiate working conditions and contracts.

- They often take care of visas and other formalities.

- In many cases, they have field offices or representatives in China, who can come to your assistance in an emergency.

- Usually, they provide some training, either back in your home country or on arrival in China, which may include a free language course.

- Sometimes, they pay the airfare.

- Sometimes, they pay for medical preparations (health checks, immunisations).

- They usually provide emergency medical care (although you or your employer have to pay for non-emergency health care).

- Some of them arrange visits by representatives, which can be a relief especially if you are based in a remote place far from another western soul who understands your western way of thinking!

Disadvantages

- Every organisation has its own philosophy (eg based on Christian belief) and rules (eg dress codes), which you have to follow whether you like them or not. If you feel uncomfortable with the rules and philosophy, it is better to go solo—or to find another organisation.

- Some sending agencies recruit only volunteers, who receive only a nominal salary (usually just enough to live on).

- Most organisations recruit only people with particular skills or qualifications (eg English teachers).

- You will find that you have two bosses—your Chinese employer as well as your field officer or China desk officer at the sending agency.

- Some organisations actually demand that you contribute towards the cost of the posting (which you should only accept if it is a charity, and if you can afford it).

- You have to commit yourself for a specified period—usually one or two years, with little flexibility to negotiate shorter or longer periods, or to change jobs.

The British Council

A UK organisation which recruits staff for China is the British Council. In addition to ELT jobs, it recruits candidates for senior lecturers' posts.

Andrea Fraser, desk officer of the Overseas Appointments Service, explains: 'Minimum qualifications are an MA in Applied Linguistics and five years' overseas experience. The contract period is usually for one year. The salary paid on average is £12,000 per annum, 11 per cent of the salary as superannuation compensation, and free accommodation. In general, the Chinese employer pays the airfare.

Vacancies are advertised in the UK national press and in the newspaper *Overseas Jobs Express.*

For information about the British Council's activities in China, you can contact the Beijing office of the British Embassy, Cultural and Education Section, 4th Floor Landmark Building, 8 North Dongsanhuan Road, Chaoyang District, Beijing 100026. Tel: (01) 501 1903. Fax: (01) 501 1977.

To find out about overseas appointments, vacancies, terms and conditions, you should contact the following address: The British Council, Overseas Appointment Services, Medlock Street, Manchester M15 4AA. Tel: (0161) 957 7000. Fax: (0161) 957 7111.

Voluntary Service Overseas

At present, VSO has about 160 volunteers in the People's Republic of China—more than in any other country—and is constantly recruiting more. In fact, there are far more VSO-approved vacancies in China than suitable candidates!

The majority of postings are for teachers and require one of the following:

- a language degree
- teaching experience
- a recognised TEFL certificate
- training and experience in a technical skills area

In addition, it helps if you have experience in teaching speaking and listening skills or methodology, and speak Chinese (Mandarin).

As well as English teachers, VSO often recruits experts in other skills areas. Recent vacancies included: a lecturer in reinforced concrete, a vegetable production expert, a women's development expert, an urban design teacher, and an accountancy teacher.

The jobs list depends on requests from prospective employers and varies from year to year. VSO acts as a recruitment, selection and sending agency. Chinese institutions and companies are the employers. Most postings are for two years.

VSO and the Chinese employer pay for:

- some training courses in the UK and in Beijing, including basic language training
- immunisations, health check, chest X-ray and Aids test, medical emergency cover
- the airfare to Beijing and a train ticket to the work placement
- a monthly salary, comparable to that of a senior teacher in China, at present 1,200 yuan (just enough to live on, but not enough for extensive travel or to keep up financial commitments at home)
- a handbook on how to teach English in China, based on the experiences of previous VSO teachers
- a Chinese language course book, targeted at the needs of foreign volunteers in China

Sometimes couples can get postings together, but VSO no longer accepts volunteers who wish to take non-volunteer partners or dependent children with them. Application forms are available from: VSO Head Office, 317 Putney Bridge Road, London SW15 2PN. Tel: (0181) 780 2266. Fax: (0181) 780 1326.

The Project Trust

Young people who want to spend a year abroad after their A levels can apply for a posting as volunteer teaching assistant with Project. This Scottish organisation acts as a selection and sending agency for young British A level educated people, and offers one year in various countries.

At present, only about fifteen volunteers are sent to China per year, but director Nicholas Maclean-Bristol says: 'We are looking closely at expanding to China.' It is likely that there will be about 100 placements per year in the near future.

Candidates must be between seventeen years, three months and nineteen years, six months old when taking up their work abroad, so it is advisable to apply early. Jay Lloyd-Smith of the China desk suggests: 'Get in touch during your first A level year.'

Nicholas Maclean-Bristol explains why they take only this one age group: 'We used to have recruits up to 23, and found we had more problems. Because our present volunteers are so young, they are more easily regarded as part of the community, and looked after very well by the locals because of their age.'

On average, about 1,500–2,000 people apply every year. 280 candidates are invited to attend a selection course, and about 200 are chosen. During the selection course, the candidates participate in a range of activities indoors and outdoors, single and in groups, and live with local families. This gives the Trust Fund a clear idea how well the candidates can adapt to a different environment, and how well they fit into a community, as well as how much they would benefit from a year overseas. The selected volunteers then attend a one-week training course.

In China, most volunteers are assistant teachers of English, teaching mostly conversation and running 'English Corners'. Nicholas Maclean-Bristol finds that it is no problem that the volunteers are inexperienced and unqualified: 'Of course, when finding a placement, we always stress how old the candidate is, to avoid wrong expectations.'

Volunteers going to China with Project receive the following:

- free accommodation and meals during the selection course
- free job-related training course (expenses paid)
- comprehensive advice on how to prepare for China
- all visa formalities taken care of
- airfare paid (included in funds to be raised)
- comprehensive emergency health care
- accommodation in China

- a monthly allowance similar to the salary of a junior teacher in China, at present 500–700 yuan
- two visits by Project representatives during the year
- regular letters from their postings officer in the UK

Volunteers have to provide the following:

- Travel to Scotland to attend selection course.
- A £100 deposit to attend the selection course. £50 of it will be refunded if you are not selected. If you are selected, the money will count towards the funds you have to raise.
- £2,950 towards the costs of their posting.

Address: The Project Trust, The Hebridean Centre, Isle of Coll, Argyll, Scotland, PA78 6TE. Tel: (018793) 444. Fax: (018793) 357.

The Amity Foundation

English teachers only are recruited by The Amity Foundation, which acts as a recruitment agency. The minimum qualification is a college degree, a BS or another high-education background.

The monthly earnings are between US$300 and US$325, and the airfare is paid by either the sending agencies or the Chinese employer. Contracts are usually for a period of one or two years.

Information is available from individual church agencies in individual countries, including the USA, Canada, the UK and Germany. If you cannot obtain information through these sources, write with an international reply coupon to: The Amity Foundation, 17 Da Jian Yin Xiang, Nanjing, China.

The Royal Society

Scientists in the fields of natural sciences, mathematics, engineering, agricultural and non-clinical medical research, psychology, archaeology and geography can apply for grants for exchange visits to China and Hong Kong.

Address: China Exchanges, The Royal Society, 6 Carlton House Terrace, London SW1Y 5AG.

BESO

British Executive Service Overseas sends highly qualified consultants to developing countries, including China. These are volunteers who undertake advisory and training assignments. Because the placements are short term (between one week and several months) BESO is of interest to retired and freelance experts rather than those seeking long term employment.

Volunteers are selected via a register. If you are interested, you can send in an application form along with your CV. If you are considered suitable (that is, if you have enough experience) you are placed on the BESO register, which currently lists 3,300 volunteers. Everyone is assigned skill codes, for example bee keeping, banking etc.

Lucien Harrington of BESO explains: 'When our recruiters receive a request for assistance, the requirements are entered on the computer, and the database prints out a list of suitable volunteers. These are then contacted to see if they are available. The volunteer's CV is sent to the company, and if they agree, dates and travel arrangements can be planned.'

Only organisations who cannot afford a commercial consultant and who are not foreign owned are considered, and assignments must contribute to the general well being of the local population and be environmentally friendly. Recent China assignments included 'non-ferrous metal fabrication', 'plastic injection moulding', 'yarn spinning and dying', 'soil conservation and improvement' and 'biscuit production adviser'.

Travel and accommodation costs are met either by the requesting organisation or by BESO.

Address: British Executive Service Overseas, 164 Vauxhall Bridge Road, London SW1V 2RB. Tel: (0171) 630 0644. Fax: (0171) 630 0624.

YMCA

If you are a citizen of an English-speaking country, have a first degree, are in good health and speak English fluently without a regional accent, the YMCA teaching programme could be of interest to you. Every year, there are between 20 and 25 openings in Taiwan.

The basic stipend covers daily living expenses. For the first six months, it is NT$13,000 per month, for the second six months NT$15,000. One year is the normal duration of stay. There are bonuses for teachers who are placed in Taipei, Taipei Country or Taichung, where the living costs are slightly higher than elsewhere, and also for those who teach more than 14 hours a week.

Housing is arranged through the YMCA in the form of a homestay with a family or a modest apartment. An allowance for housing in addition to the monthly stipend is provided by the YMCA. The YMCA arranges medical insurance and pays for special training, as well as for in-country language courses in Mandarin Chinese. There is also a vacation bonus, and taxes are paid by the YMCA.

Teachers have to pay their own airfare to Taiwan. The YMCA pays for the airfare back.

The catch is that this programme has been designed with American applicants in mind. Although candidates from other English-speaking countries are positively encouraged, they must be in North America from the application deadline until they leave for Taiwan, to attend interviews and a special training course.

Application deadline is 15 April, but earlier applications are welcome. Departure date is September.

For a detailed information leaflet, write to: International Office for Asia, YMCA of the USA, OSCY, 909–4th Ave, Seattle, Washington 98104. Tel: (206) 382 5008. Fax: (206) 382 7283.

GOING SOLO

If you prefer being independent and flexible, and have bags of initiative, diplomacy and patience, there's nothing to stop you from finding a job on your own.

Making contact

You can get in touch with prospective employers directly, sending application letters on spec. You may be able to get addresses of companies and institutions which relate to your skills area from the Chinese embassy in your country, from the Chinese Association for the International Exchange of Personnel, or from international trade organisations.

However, be prepared to wait for a long time until you receive a reply—if you get one at all. Everything foreign tends to be regarded as complicated and important, and therefore put aside until someone comes up with a suitably bureaucratic procedure.

Many application letters are never retrieved from the pile of 'important' matters . . .

You may have to send out two dozen or more application letters to receive a single reply.

If at all possible, try and get a personal introduction or letter of recommendation from someone who knows both you and the prospective employer. This will not guarantee you a job, but it will guarantee that your application will be read.

If you know someone who is living in China, ask them to make contact with, for example, college headmasters, and then mention your availability. Your chances of finding a job will increase 1,000 per cent.

Chinese educational institutions which regularly employ foreign teachers include:

- Beijing University, Haidian District, Beijing. Tel: (01) 282 471. This is China's most prestigious university, and employs forty or more foreign teachers in various departments. Teachers must be highly qualified, and are treated well. Good accommodation is provided. Contact the Foreign Affairs Office.

- Beijing University of Post and Telecommunications (Zhongguo Beijing Youdian Daxue, 213 Xinxiang, Beijing. Tel: (01) 326 0993). This institution has only recently achieved university status, and employs two or more foreign teachers every year, usually to teach English conversation. Accommodation on the college campus is provided (two rooms, plus kitchen and bathroom). Contact the Foreign Affairs Office.

The following language schools in Taiwan are recruiting teachers:

- ELSI Taiwan Language School, Head Office, 12 Kuling Street, Taipei, Taiwan. Tel: (02) 321 9005, 394 2304. This school has an adults' programme (for students aged 14–60), as well as a children's programme (4–13). Basic and pronunciation classes are taught by native Chinese instructors, but the intensive, basic, writing, conversation and business classes are taught by native English speakers.

The current faculty includes almost 300 teachers from nine

countries, most of whom teach between 12 and 20 hours per week. A few teachers have been with the school since it opened in 1982, and many others have stayed for more than two years.

'We use an organised but flexible curriculum, focusing on student-centered methodologies,' explains the school's leaflet. 'Though the syllabuses are detailed, teachers have a great deal of freedom in interpreting materials and structuring classes to meet their students' specific needs.'

Payment is NT$390 per hour for daytime teaching, and NT$420 per hour for evening and weekend teaching. The school points out a peculiarity of the Taiwan tax sysyem: 'For the first six months you are in Taiwan, national income tax regulations require the school to withhold 20 per cent of your income, but most of the withholding is refunded when you file a tax return for the year. However, to get a tax refund, you must establish de facto residency in Taiwan by staying on the island at least 183 days during the calendar year, which means that if you arrive after 2 July, you will not get a refund on the 20 per cent withholding.'

Applicants have to pay their own airfare to Taiwan. Luisa Sia, the administrative director, says: 'All interviews and hiring are done in Taiwan. We will decide after an interview and observation of classes.'

This means, of course, that no job is guaranteed. You have to travel to Taiwan and hope that, if ELSI doesn't want your services, another school does.

Applicants must have a college diploma, BSC or BA degree, be prepared to stay for at least one year, and, if possible, have experience in teaching English as a foreign language. Only passport holders from native English-speaking countries (including USA, Canada, UK, Australia, South Africa, Singapore and New Zealand) will be considered. Luisa Sia says: 'The whole application process takes about one month after you submit your paperwork to us.'

- One of the biggest language schools in Taiwan is constantly recruiting English teachers: Hess Language School, Po Ai Road, No83 2F Taipei, Taiwan. Tel: (02) 383 5440. Fax: (02) 382 0799. Recruits must be university graduates, and contracts are for one year. Accommodation is not provided, but the school offers to help locate suitable accommodation.

Writing application letters

When applying for a job, either on spec or in reply to an advertisement, enclose as many certificates as possible—they increase your status. Mention your main skills and experiences in the application letter as well as in your CV. Chinese employers tend to pay more attention to the application letter than to the CV.

Qualifications mentioned only in the CV may go unnoticed. In a country where it is still the norm to trade job vacancies for guanxi (ie the best-connected, not the best-qualified candidate gets a job), employers are not used to reading CVs, and may not understand them. When enclosing a CV, avoid the brief, tabular form. Send a piece of detailed prose instead.

JOBHUNTING ON THE SPOT

Finding a job while in China

Another possibility is simply to travel to China, and go jobhunting there.

'You can just stand at Beijing Railway Station, carrying a sign 'I want to be an English teacher', and you'll have a job within a few days,' says Philip, who has been teaching English in China for two years.

Even native Chinese teachers use this method to find side jobs. People carrying signs such as 'I teach Russian, Japanese, Arts . . .' can be found in most cities.

The problem is, of course, that without a visa you cannot work legally in China, and once you are in China, it's virtually impossible to get a visa.

A possible solution is to leave China and to apply from a neighbouring country. But of course, there are no guarantees that your visa application will succeed.

Picking up casual work

Casual work is easy to find. Indeed, most foreigners working in China find that they are offered casual jobs, especially when they are travelling. Most of them are not interested in taking on extra work, because spare time is more precious than a few yuan per evening.

However, this option can be of interest to people who want to see China as tourists rather than work there full time, and who want to add to their budget by doing casual work.

But bear in mind that taking on paid work when you are in the country as a tourist is illegal! The decision is yours, but you have been warned.

Wealthy families sometimes require part time governesses or tutors to prepare their children for English exams. They are often able to pay good money (10 yuan or more per hour), but it's unlikely that you will get a visa for employment with a private family. Of course you can always strike a deal such as 'one meal for one lesson', and sample Chinese family life.

It is safer to be paid in goods or services instead of money. For example, the deal 'ten English lessons for ten Chinese lessons' is no problem.

A couple of Brits were hired to take part in a TV commercial for tea, and received one year's supply of tea. An Irishman attended a trade fair as a living advertisement for technical products 'made to western standards', and got board and lodging in a good hotel for the duration of the fair, as well as a train ticket to his next destination in China.

CASE STUDIES

Fiona applies for a teaching job

Twenty-eight-year-old Fiona is already working in her third job in China. With an MA in Chinese, an MSc in applied linguistics and a TEFL certificate on top of it, she has no difficulty finding teaching jobs in China.

'My long-term career plans were only a secondary factor,' she says. 'I wanted to do something with my language skills. Three years after graduation, I had not spoken any Chinese. I wanted to be in a situation to improve my Chinese. The only way was to go to China, either as a student, which I could not afford, or as a teacher, which I did.'

She was staying in Thailand when friends told her about a vacancy at Qingdao Ocean University. She applied, was accepted, braved a flood of forms and visa requirements and taught English for a year.

'Then I was offered a job at Qingdao Foreign Trade College

and worked there for half a year. When you've been teaching in China for a while, you'll get many job offers.'

She returned to Scotland to continue her studies. When she was ready to go to China again, she picked Baishan, a picturesque town in the northeast, to live and work. At first she tried to apply directly to the teaching institutions there, but received no reply. So she applied with VSO, was accepted, and because of her outstanding qualifications, was posted to the destination of her choice, where she is now teaching at the Education College.

'When I went on my own, I received a higher salary than I do now as a volunteer, but I had to pay my own airfare, so on the whole it's about the same.'

Sarah joins the VSO

Sarah, 22, who wanted to become an actress initially, went to drama college, then obtained a teaching degree and decided that teaching was her true vocation.

'I wanted some world experience,' she explains. 'Also, my convent school education was very community based. It taught me to care about people, and help them. I feel that having had a good life already, I want to give something, too.'

Most projects were Christianity-based. Although she has a strong faith, she feels that working for a religious organisation would have limited her.

'The other problem was that most organisations accepted only people who were 25 or older. So I applied with VSO, although they required two years commitment.'

However, VSO needed people who could teach English, not drama, so she had to gain a TEFL qualification. 'The course taught me a lot about lesson planning, although much of what I learnt was more geared towards teaching in a well equipped western school.'

Sarah did not choose China. 'It just happened that VSO had more vacancies in China than anywhere else, and because I'm not an experienced teacher I had to take what was offered. But the China posting provided me with exactly the personal challenge I had hoped for.'

She finds that her acting skills help her with her daily work: 'To some extent, teaching is acting, I am playing a role in the classroom. My drama background gives me confidence and helps me devise role plays, which the students enjoy.'

Layla joins the Project Trust

After finishing her A levels, Layla opted for a year overseas to widen her horizon. For her, too, the destination just happened—but she 'fell in love with China'.

Layla found that everything was made easy for her: 'The job was completely set up for me by Project Trust, who suggested that I could go to China to teach at a middle school. They also chose who my partner would be for the year, which worked out perfectly. Project Trust gave us all the information we needed about what to take with us, as they had the experience of having people there before. I went over-prepared rather than under-prepared.'

3
Getting Ready

OBTAINING A VISA

For a visa, write to the relevant embassy in your home country to obtain a visa form, a health form and an up-to-date list of documents needed. Requirements for tourist visas and for work or study visas differ. Apply well in advance—there may be complications which delay the visa. Make sure, too, that you have a passport which is valid for at least the planned duration of your stay; otherwise the embassy will refuse to give you a visa.

These documents are needed for the PR China:

- For a tourist visa: a completed application form, two passport photographs, and valid passport with blank pages.

- For a tourist visa to Tibet: a completed application form, two passport photographs, a valid passport with blank pages and written approval by the Tourist Bureau of Tibet which can be contacted on Fax 86 891 34632.

- For business and long-term work visas: a completed application form, two passport photographs, a valid passport with blank pages, a letter of invitation from the Chinese government or government-authorised Chinese company, and, if staying longer than six months, a health certificate.

- For student visas: a completed application form, two passport photographs, a valid passport with blank pages, a special visa application form for international students (JW-202) issued by the State Education Commission of China, a notification of admission from the receiving college with the seal of the commission and, if staying longer than six months, a health certificate.

At the Chinese Embassy in London, British passport holders are charged £25 for a single visa, which has to be paid in cash or by postal order; cheques are not accepted. Visa applications submitted in person take three working days to process (Monday–Friday, 9.00–12.00). Those sent by mail are treated as low priority, take 15 days plus mailing time, and cost £10 more.

Address: Embassy of the People's Republic of China, 31 Portland Place, London W1N 3AG. Tel: (0171) 636 1835.

The health certificate

You must obtain a form for a *Physical Examination Record for Foreigner* from the embassy, and ask your doctor to fill it in. It covers such vital questions about how the doctor judges your 'state of neck', 'colour sense' and 'nourishment', and if you suffer from 'mental confusion, endangering the public order and security'.

You will have to pay your doctor for the check-up. In addition, the health form requires your doctor's confirmation that you are free from Aids, venereal diseases and lung infections, which means that you have to pay for laboratory tests and a chest X-ray as well.

In some hospitals, you can simply walk in and have a chest X-ray done; in others, your doctor has to arrange for an appointment and you may have to wait weeks to get one. This can mean a considerable delay to your visa application, so get these things done as early as possible.

These documents are needed for Taiwan

Applicants for a single entry visa must produce a completed application form (see Fig. 2), a passport valid for at least six months, two passport-sized photographs, and documents verifying the purpose of the visit, or evidence of a sponsor in the Republic of China (usually your employer, if you have one, or a resident of Taiwan), and a fee of £12.50.

Health tests, including an Aids test are needed as well, but regulations demand that they are done on arrival in Taiwan. Contact the Taiwan Embassy in your home country for up-to-date details.

Address: Taipei Representative Office in the UK, 50 Grosvenor Gardens, London WS1W 0EB. Tel: (0171) 396 9152. Fax: (0171)

396 9145. Or: Travel Documents Handling Unit. Tel: (0171) 396 9143. Fax: (0171) 396 9144.

PACKING YOUR SUITCASE

Unless you are in the lucky position that your employer or sending organisation pays for extra luggage, you will have only a tight luggage allowance. You can take only a fraction of the things you think you really need!

The good news is that nowadays all really essential items are available in Beijing and other big cities.

Clothing is good and cheap, but you may have problems getting it in large sizes. Cotton and wool are rarely used. The Chinese consider acrylics and nylon to be far superior. We westerners may not agree with that, when we work in the sweltering heat of the south with synthetic clothing sticking to our sweaty bodies, or if we have to wear several layer of underwear to keep us warm in the chilly north and our skin can't breathe. Of course, the Chinese have the advantage that their bodies sweat and smell less than the westerners.

So take some cotton underwear and cotton or woollen socks. Pack at least two complete sets of thermal underwear and socks, too, wherever you go. In the north, it is ice cold and you will be wearing several layers. Even in the south, it can get extremely cold on occasions, and the south has no central heating.

Chinese tailors are very skilled and can copy any item of clothing quite cheaply. Many westerners take one set of clothing (eg one skirt, one blouse, one pair of trousers, etc), buy the material, and have duplicates made in a variety of colours. The drawback is, of course, that it's all synthetics again.

You won't be able to buy a bra in anything larger than size A. Shoes are a problem, too, if you are a woman with feet larger than size five or a man with feet larger than size eight. As a woman, you can buy men's walking shoes. If you are going to the north, you will need to take water and mud-proof thermal boots, but you can buy a warm padded or down jacket at a surprisingly low price.

Pens, paper and stationery are all readily available and cheap, although not always of good quality. Pencils tend to break. Sticky tape, a few years ago worth its weight in gold, can now be bought

填表前請詳閱背頁注意事項
Please read the overleaf NOTE before completing this form

本表格係免費供應
This form is given FREE OF CHARGE

核發機關填註 FOR OFFICE USE ONLY

□面談 □核准 □未面談 □拒絕
□停留 □居留 □外交 □禮遇 □單次 □多次

備註
簽證號碼
核准停留期限
簽發日期
簽證官員簽字
費用

三個月內半身近照兩張
Please attach 2 recent bust photos (taken within last three months)

簽證申請表 VISA APPLICATION FORM FOR ENTRY INTO THE REPUBLIC OF CHINA

FORM -V-1 (Please print or typewrite)

擬申請何種簽證 WHICH CATEGORY OF VISA ARE YOU APPLYING FOR?

1. 種類: Category □停留簽證 Visitor visa □居留簽證 Resident visa □外交簽證 Diplomatic visa □禮遇簽證 Courtesy visa

2. 入境次數: Entry □單次 Single □多次 Multiple

申請人資料 APPLICANT'S DETAILS:

姓 Surname 名 Given and middle name(s)

3. 全名(與護照所載相同): Full name (extactly as in passport)

4. 中文姓名(如有的話): Chinese name (if any)

5. 曾有或其他姓名(如有的話): Former or other name (if any)

6. 性別: Sex □男 Male □女 Female

7. 婚姻狀況: Marital status □未婚 Single □已婚 Married □鰥寡 Widowed □分居 Separated □離婚 Divorced

8. 出生日期: Date of birth 日(Day) 月(Month) 年(Year)

9. 出生地點: Place of birth 市(City) 國(Country)

10. 國籍: Nationality

11. 曾有或其他國籍(如有的話): Former or other nationality (if any)

12. 現在住址: Present address ☎

13. 永久住址(如異於12): Permanent address (if different from 12)

14. 職業: Occupation

15. 服務機關或就讀學校: Name of employer or school ☎

申請人護照 APPLICANT'S PASSPORT:

16. 種類: Type □外交 Diplomatic □公務 Official □普通 Regular □其他: 請指明: Other; please specify

17. 號碼: No.

18. 發照地點: Place of issue

19. 發照日期: Date of issue

20. 效期屆滿日: Date of expiry

21. 與申請人持同一護照之同行眷屬: Accompanying dependent(s) included in passport

姓名 Name	出生日期 Date of birth	與申請人關係 Relationship to applicant

訪華行程 JOURNEY TO TAIWAN, R. O. C.:

22. 訪華目的: Purpose of journey □旅遊 Tourism □洽商 Business □過境 Transit □參加會議(請指明): Attending a meeting (specify) □應聘 Empolyment □依親 Joining family □其他:(請指明): Other; (specify)

23. 預定抵華日期: Proposed date of arrival 日(Day) 月(Month) 年(Year)

24. 預定停留時間: Length of intended stay 年 Years 月 Months 日 Days

25. 抵華後住址: Address during the intended stay

26. 在華關係人: Reference in Taiwan, R. O. C. 姓名 Name 與申請人關係 Relationship to applicant

27. 住址 Address 電話號碼 Telephone No.

Fig. 2. Visa application form for Taiwan.

請據實回答以下問題 PLEASE ANSWER THE FOLLOWING QUESTIONS ACCORDING TO FACT :

27 你是否曾遭中華民國驅逐出境？
Have you ever been deported from Taiwan, R.O.C.?
☐ 是 Yes ☐ 否 No 如果是，何時？何原因？ If Yes, when and why

28 你是否曾遭中華民國駐外代表機構拒發簽證？
Have you ever been refused a visa at a mission of Taiwan, R.O.C.?
☐ 是 Yes ☐ 否 No 如果是，何時？何處？ If Yes, when and where

29 近兩年你是否曾赴中華民國？
Have you been to Taiwan, R.O.C. within the last two years?
☐ 是 Yes ☐ 否 No 如果是，何時？何原因？ If Yes, when and why

茲聲明：本人瞭解申請表各節，且所填資料均屬真實。
Declaration I understand all the notes and questions in this application and the information furnished above is true and complete.

申請人簽名：
Signature of applicant

申請日期：
Date of application

日 (Day) 月 (Month) 年 (Year)

本人係應申請人委託代填申請表。
I have completed this application at the request of the applicant

代理人簽名：
Signature of agent

代理人全名及住址：
Agent's full name and address

與申請人關係：
Relationship to applicant

注意事項 NOTE :

■隨行兒童倘持用同一護照，可於本表中與你一同提出簽證申請；其他申請人則需另填表格。
You can include children in this application if they are included in your passport and traveling 'with you; every other person must complete a separate application form.

■任何虛偽或不明確之陳述均可能使簽證申請遭到拒絕。
If you make any false or indistinct statements, you commit an offence and your application may be declined.

■簽證持有人倘屬禁止入境者，或其簽證係用不當方法取得者，仍無權進入中華民國。
You should understand that possession of a visa does not entitle you to enter the Republic of China upon arrival at port of entry if you are found otherwise inadmissible or if the visa is fraudulently obtained.

■中華民國政府有權不透露拒發簽證之原因。
You should also understand that the Government of the Republic of China reserves the right to withhold the reason for the disapproval of any visa application.

■非經事前申請許可，不得在中華民國境內工作。
You are not permitted to accept employment in the Republic of China without prior approval.

■因過境、觀光、探親、訪問、研習、洽辦工商業務或因其他事務而擬在中華民國境內作六個月以下停留者，請選填申請停留簽證。
Please choose to apply for a VISITOR VISA, if you intend to stay in the Republic of China for less than six months for the purpose of transit, sightseeing, visiting relatives, or conducting business or other activities.

■停留期限為六十天者，抵華後可於期限屆滿前，檢具有關文件向停留地縣、市警察局申請延長停留，每次得停留六十天，以二次為限。停留期限為二星期、三十天、或六十天並加註「不得延期」戳記者，非因不可抗力或其他重大事故，不得申請延期。
With a visitor visa, you may stay in the Republic of China for sixty days and may, on good grounds, apply at the nearest city/county police headquarters for a maximum of two extensions, each for sixty days. No extension of stay will be granted if the duration of stay is restricted to two weeks, thirty days, or sixty days with a restrictive stamp of "No Extension Will Be Granted", except for situation caused by force majeure or matter of vital importance.

■因依親、就學、應聘、投資、就醫、傳教或從事其他業務，而擬在中華民國境內作六個月以上居留者，請選填申請居留簽證。
Please choose to apply for a RESIDENT VISA, if you intend to stay in the Republic of China for more than six months for the purpose of joining family, pursuing studies, accepting employment, making investment, receiving medical treatment, doing missionary work, or engaging in other activities.

■持居留簽證來華者，須於入境後十五天內向居留地縣、市警察局申請外僑居留證。
Holding a resident visa, you are required to apply for an Alien Resident Certificate at the city/county police headquarters within fifteen days after entry into the Republic of China.

in every department store and street market. Correction fluid and blutack, however, are still difficult to find.

Gluesticks are very useful—Chinese glue is a sticky, messy, unpractical affair. Take typewriter ribbons and special batteries for your camera. Slide film is difficult to obtain outside Beijing, but print film can be bought in most towns.

The selection of cosmetics is becoming wider, too. Chinese cosmetics are of good quality, although heavily perfumed. Soaps are especially good, and pleasantly fragranced. Hand creams are good but so strongly perfumed that your hands smell for hours, at a distance of twenty metres! In the large cities, department stores sell Nivea cream and body lotion.

Among western cosmetics, Ponds is best represented. In fact, department stores in Chinese cities offer a wider variety of Ponds face creams and moisturisers than the average High Street Boots shop in the UK. Experiment with Ponds moisturisers at home, find a suitable one, and buy it in China.

Bear in mind, however, that in a different climate your skin will have different requirements. In the dry cold northeast, for example, you will need a stronger moisturiser or face cream than at home.

Lip salve used to be hard to get, but is available in Beijing and northern cities, so you need not bring your own supplies.

Chinese toothpaste contains sugar! However, some western brands such as Colgate can be bought in department stores in the big cities. Tampons are increasingly available in provincial capitals and industrial towns, but if you travel through Beijing you may want to stock up there, just in case. Tampons are a little cheaper in Beijing than in the west. Paper tissues are spreading slowly and cost about the same as in the west.

Some westerners wished they had brought cotton ear buds—the Chinese use metal hooks to clean their ears.

Moist baby wipes and feminine tissues are extremely useful for adults, male or female, especially when travelling. Most public toilets have neither loo paper nor water to wash your hands.

The quality of Chinese vitamin tablets varies, so bring your own. For other medicines, see chapter 10 'Staying Healthy'.

Don't forget to take your address book (leave a photocopy at home, just in case it gets lost), photos of your friends, family and home town to show to your new Chinese friends, posters of the UK to decorate the classroom or your flat, and a personal alarm.

Knives, spoons and forks can be bought in cities, although of a poor quality. You may want to take some room fragrance with you, because Chinese sanitation is poor and it can be difficult to get rid of the smell in the bathroom.

Books in English language are difficult to get, with the exception of classics (especially Mark Twain and Charles Dickens, who represent the cause of the workers), which can be bought in foreign language bookstores in provincial capitals. For teaching materials, see chapter 8 'Teaching English'. You can send books and magazines by post as printed matter; it's cheaper than paying for excess luggage.

Take some stamps and postcards (especially sights of London with red double decker buses) which make useful small gifts.

All essential foodstuffs can be bought in China. Milk is rare, but milk powder is available. You may want to take some baking powder, powdered soup and sauces, curry and dried French or Italian herb mixes. Instant coffee, including Nescafé, is available from big department stores.

Torches, standard size batteries, adapters, hair dryers, towels, shortwave radios, tape recorders, and cameras can all be bought in China.

Chinese-English dictionaries are much cheaper in Beijing than in the west, but they are not as good. If you plan to use your dictionary a lot, take one with you. Otherwise, you can get the red *Concise English–Chinese Chinese–English Dictionary* at the Foreign Language Bookstore in Beijing for as little as 14 yuan (about £1). It is compact in size and contains an incredible amount of vocabulary (except the words you really need).

A very good, large map of China in English language is also available at the Foreign Language Bookstore and costs only 7 yuan (50 pence).

Case study

Heather writes from Xingyi: 'I've had a lot of clothes made by a local tailor and am generally very satisfied with the results. I wish I'd brought more shoes with me, as I take size 8. My Chinese shoes (which I bought in England, export size) have already fallen to pieces. I'm having some pairs sent over. I wish I had brought a Mickey Mouse mask, to give people a reason for that stupid grin on their faces . . .'

What to take to China

Item	Bring from home	Buy in Beijing	Buy at placement
Clothing			
Thermal underwear	●		
Thermal socks	●		
Cottons socks	●		
Woollen socks	●		
Warm silk underwear (small sizes)		●	
Warm padded jacket		●	●
Jumpers (acrylic)		●	●
Jumpers (wool)	●		
Cotton underwear	●		
Bras (above size A)	●		
Shirts and blouses	●	●	●
Skirts and trousers	●	●	●
Thermal gloves	●		
Warm hat			●
Shoes (small sizes)			●
Shoes (large sizes)	●		
Moonboots	●		
Food			
Powdered soup	●		
Oxo cubes	●		
Instant coffee			●
Curry	●		
Italian herbs	●		
Dried herbs			●
Foodstuff general			●
Good chocolate		●	
Low quality chocolate			●
Biscuits			●

Fig. 3. Checklist: What to take to China.

What to take to China

Item	Bring from home	Buy in Beijing	Buy at placement
Medicines			
Plasters	●	●	●
Bandages	●		
Syringes and needles	●		
Vitam tablets	●		
Travel sickness tablets	●		
Malaria tablets	●		
Cold remedies	●		●
Diarrhea remedies	●		●
Gifts			
Illustrated books of your home country	●		
Postage stamps of your home country	●		
Photography			
Good camera	●		
Cheap camera		●	
Print film		●	●
Slide film	●	●	
Batteries for camera	●		
Stationery			
Correction fluid	●		
Self-adhesive tape			●
Typewriter ribbon	●		
Good typewriter	●		
Gluestick	●		
Blutack	●		
Pens, pencils, paper and envelopes			●

What to take to China

Item	Bring from home	Buy in Beijing	Buy at placement
Books			
Dictionary	●	●	
Classics		●	
Contemporary	●		
Map of China		●	
Map of your home country	●		
China guidebook	●		
For your flat			
Torch			●
Hairdryer			●
Room fragrance	●		
Cutlery		●	
Crockery			●
Bedding, towels			●
Adapter		●	
Shortwave radio		●	
Tape recorder		●	
Batteries, standard			●
Alarmclock			●
Cosmetics			
Lipsalve		●	
Moisturiser		●	●
Handcream	●	●	●
Feminine tissues	●		
Toothpaste		●	
Tampons		●	
Earbuds	●		
Shaving gear	●	●	●

What to take to China

Item	Bring from home	Buy in Beijing	Buy at placement
Cosmetics continued			
Soap			●
Unperfumed shampoo		●	
Unperfumed handcream		●	
Unperfumed soap	●		
Good perfume	●	●	
Cheap sweet perfume		●	●
Other items			
Personal alarm	●		
Blank tapes		●	●
Western music tapes	●	●	
Swiss army knife	●	●	
Guitar		●	
Posters of your home country	●		
Postcards of your home country	●		
Small gifts, typical of your home country	●		
Don't forget			
Passport	●		
Vaccination record	●		
Blood test lab results (Aids, venereal diseases, blood group)	●		
Health certificate	●		
Address book	●		
Photos	●		

Checklist

The checklist in Fig. 3 has been compiled with the advice of foreigners presently in China. It applies to the People's Republic of China only, and it shows the best/cheapest/easiest place where to obtain things, but this does not mean that this is the only way.

Naturally, the decision on what to take depends on where you will be going, your personal circumstances and the type of work you do.

LEARNING THE LANGUAGE

Learning Chinese before you go

Several adult education centres offer Chinese language classes for beginners. If you live in London, you can also contact the Great Britain–China Centre (15 Belgrave Square, London, SW1X 8PS. Tel: (0171) 235 6696. Fax: (0171) 245 6885) which organises Chinese evening classes.

If you have limited time, or want a more flexible approach to your studies, there are excellent tape courses available (eg from Linguaphone or BBC).

It is said that the best way to learn a language is in the country itself. However, many westerners in China wish they had started learning the language at home. The Chinese language, especially the pronunciation and intonation, is so different from European languages, that most students find it difficult at first. You will be grateful for every bit you've learnt because it gives you a better start.

Studying the language in country

Unfortunately, there are few organised Chinese language courses in China, and the reports about them are not always favourable.

'My teacher spent hours teaching me how to draw semi circles and upward strokes,' reports one student. 'I didn't have a clue what she was trying to achieve. It was only several weeks later that I realised she was doing preliminary exercises for teaching me the Latin alphabet! She had a degree in English, but hadn't realised that as a native English speaker I would be able to write the Latin alphabet which is needed for Chinese Pinyin.'

If you enrol for a course, make sure that your tutor has had experience in teaching other foreigners.

On average, language classes in Taiwan are better organised; contact the embassy of Taiwan for details.

Mandarin Chinese (putonghua) is the standard Chinese written and spoken in most parts of PR China. However, the dialects are so different that people from different provinces often cannot understand each other. If you want to learn pure Mandarin Chinese, go to Beijing or to the northeast.

4
Settling In

FURNISHING YOUR FLAT

Depending on your contract, your employer is normally responsible for providing you with suitable accommodation. As a foreigner, you are likely to be allocated more living space than your Chinese colleagues.

If you have a choice of flats, choose one on the first floor. Ground floor flats are more at risk of burglaries, and any place higher than the first floor is without water as soon as the water pressure drops.

Don't accept a flat which isn't ready by the time you arrive. If there is no water and electricity by the time you arrive, chances are that there still won't be any by the time you leave . . .

Whether your flat is furnished or not, depends on your contract (see Chapter 7) Working in China.

Water supplies

Most town houses have running water. However, droughts and water shortages are frequent, and it is possible that you get water only during certain hours of the day, or no water at all for days or weeks.

Westerners who set out to live in a hot climate or near the deserts are mentally prepared for this problem—but to those living in the cold northeast this can come as a shock.

A sudden water shortage means you can't flush the toilet or clean the house, you can't wash yourself, your foodstuff, your cups and plates, your clothes, and there's nothing to drink but beer and sweet lemonade.

Store as much water as you can, in buckets, jars and tanks. Always keep the bathtub filled with water. You will not be able to have a bath, of course. But in China, a bathtub is not for bathing. It's for storing water.

What you need to know about gas and electricity

Chinese plugs and sockets throw sparks when you use them; consider it normal. But when the cables start smelling of burnt rubber and plastic, it's time to get worried.

Try and insist that a qualified electrician does all the electric wiring. Many Chinese believe they have the necessary knowledge, often with disastrous results. If you plan to do it yourself, shop around and buy the most expensive cables, plugs and sockets. They are the safest.

You will need electricity for your fridge, washing machine, rice steamer, tape recorder, radio, TV and for the lighting.

Gas, on the other hand, is safe in China. It comes in huge flasks, which you take for a refill. Warning: they are heavy. Find someone with a car who is willing to drive you to the gas refill station. Investigate where exactly you have to go to obtain a refill. By sheer coincidence, you will find that the place is either closed when you need it, or the relevant person is 'too busy', 'not there' or 'can't do it now'. A gas refill lasts about three months and costs around 30 yuan. You will be using gas mostly for cooking.

Equipping the kitchen

The typical Chinese kitchen has a gas cooker, usually with one ring only (it's amazing how the Chinese can produce a dozen dishes for a banquet with a single gas ring). Instead of saucepans and frying pans, you have a wok and a teakettle.

Buy a rice steamer as well, one which works with electricity. This gives you independence: in the case of power failure, you can still cook food in the wok, and if you run out of gas, you can cook with the electric steamer.

The main cooking utensils are a huge wooden chopping board and a chopping knife. These, as well as other items such as small kitchen knives, are available in the bigger department stores.

Buy enough rice bowls (the larger ones), and mugs with lids to entertain guests.

You need at least one of the huge thermos flasks to keep a constant supply of boiled water for drinking, making coffee and tea, and washing fruit. It is best to keep at least two flasks of hot water ready at all times. You never know when the water, electricity and gas supplies will break down at the same time.

Cupboards, tables, small baking ovens and fridges can be bought in China. Western items, such as microwaves, are available in Beijing, and sometimes in the big department stores in the provincial capital.

The bathroom

Assuming—and hoping—that you have a western style flush toilet and a bathtub for water storage, you will need a shower. Basically, this is a container for heating water which hangs on the wall. Not above the bathtub though—having a shower in the bathtub would get your drinking water dirty, wouldn't it? You stand on the bathroom floor to have a shower. There's a hole in every bathroom floor through which the water disappears.

You fill the boiler of your shower by connecting a plastic pipe to the water tap and turning the tap on. It fills up quickly if the water pressure happens to be strong enough. The boiler can store enough water for a shower and for washing your hair. Remember to keep it full at all times. It is not always possible to regulate the temperature. Most showers make it necessary to establish, by trial and error, how long it takes to achieve a comfortable temperature, eg seventeen minutes, and you must switch it off after precisely that time, or you'll get burnt.

Chinese washing machines have two drums: one for washing, one for spinning. Electric power sets them in motion. Washing machines are not connected to water pipes, so you have to fill the washing drum with several buckets of water. They can take only cold water; it is not possible to boil wash anything in them.

The washing cycle lasts about fifteen minutes, the spin cycle about seven minutes. Don't expect your clothes to be clean. Reasonable results are achieved by following this procedure: wash, spin, wash, spin, wash, spin, rinse, spin, rinse and spin. Chinese detergent (powder sold in plastic bags) is thorough but aggressive.

To drain, lead the machine's thick plastic pipe to the hole in the ground.

The Chinese drainage system does not always work very well, and many westerners report that they find their bathrooms have an unpleasant smell which they cannot get rid of. You may want to bring some room fragrance from home.

Decorating and furnishing

The Chinese like bright colours, and you may find that the way they have decorated the flat for you is not quite your taste: the lower half of the wall in dark brown, the upper in turquoise blue, with pink curtains and an orange carpet, for example.

Unless you expect to stay for several years, it's probably not worth redecorating. Most westerners achieve a pleasant atmosphere by putting up many posters, postcards and photos of their home country. Everything around you is Chinese; you need a little 'home from home' which can be very comforting when you go through periods of frustration or homesickness.

However, you can buy your own curtains and bedspreads and large pieces of material to put up on the walls.

KEEPING SAFE

'China has the lowest reported crime rate in the world'. This statement is perfectly true. But the emphasis is on the word 'reported'.

Crime happens everywhere in the world, and it is a fact that more and more foreigners in China are victims of crime. This does not mean that it is more dangerous to live in China than in most other countries, but it means that you have to be careful. Take the same precautions you would take if you went to somewhere like New York.

Wherever you go, carry your personal alarm with you. Don't go for walks on your own if you live in a rough area, especially at night-time.

Somebody has a key to your place

Your employer has a key to your place, and so have, probably, other people. You notice it when you come home one day and find that the papers on your desk and the books on your shelf are arranged differently.

If nothing has disappeared, somebody is spying on you, which is infuriating. Perhaps your employers will admit it, perhaps they won't. What are they looking for? A party representative may be looking for politically sensitive material; you could, for example, be a spy or you could be sent by your government to infiltrate unwanted political ideas. Some western teachers, especially in

Beijing, are convinced that their rooms and phones are bugged. There were also cases when the police raided foreigners' flats in their absence. These incidents, however, are becoming rarer.

Another reason is plain curiosity. What does the foreigner keep in those drawers? All the alluring secrets of the west are hidden in your flat.

The third possibility is burglary. Unfortunately, some westerners found that valuable items, especially cameras, disappeared from their flats, and there were no signs of forced entry.

How to prevent raids and burglaries

Whatever the reason for the break-ins, it is disturbing that you don't even have a little sanctuary of your own. It can make you feel helpless, furious, or insecure. This is what you can do:

- Tell your employer and colleagues that you are furious. It may not even have occurred to them that you disapprove of the raids.

- When you have visitors, even close friends, don't leave cameras and valuables lying around for everyone to see. The temptation may be too great. Or they may just happen to mention all those wonderful things you have in your flat to someone who has a key and no scruples.

- Many doors and locks discourage the casual spy or thief. Most thefts from westerners' flats were items lying around on tables, shelves and chairs. Valuables in cupboards, even if unlocked, appear to be much safer.

- As soon as you arrive, buy some padlocks at the department store and fix them to your front door, so that you can lock it from the outside. Also get a huge bolt to secure against intruders while you are in. You may want to get padlocks for several doors inside your flat to minimise the chances of someone entering with duplicate or universal keys. If somebody protests against your precautions, it shows their intention!

COPING WITH PROBLEMS

Your Chinese visitors are curious—they may take your books out of the shelves, look through your photo albums unasked, and read any letters they find on your desk.

You don't have to put up with this. They don't behave like this when visiting a Chinese teacher or colleague. Make it quite clear that you don't like it.

If you have two rooms, make one of them 'public', This is where you entertain visitors. Have plenty of photos, postcards and posters on the wall for them to look at, perhaps a few books which you don't mind them borrowing.

The second room is your sanctuary. This is where you sleep and work, where you keep your documents, letters, private photo albums and cosmetics, in short everything you don't want to disappear and would not want strangers to rummage through. Keep the door to this room closed.

Chinese don't have a concept of privacy the way westerners have. Many grew up with a family living in a one room hut. Students live in dormitories, eight to twelve people in a room. They are used to having people around them at all times, and soon feel lonely if there isn't anyone around.

For them, it's difficult to understand that a foreigner wants to be alone. They see that you are living alone, and will do their best to keep you company at all times. When you are ill they will arrange for all their friends (whom you've never seen before) to sit in your bedroom. It depends on your mentality, but most westerners, when they are ill, want to be left alone! You must explain this tactfully.

The only reason the Chinese can understand for your odd request to be left alone is that you are 'very busy'. If you want peace you can say, 'I'm sorry, I'm very busy just now. I would like you to visit me again another day. Would you like to come tomorrow?'

Some westerners found it useful to put up a note on their door, saying 'Thank you for coming to see me. I am sorry I am very tired at the moment and need to rest' (or 'I'm very busy at the moment and cannot have visitors'). 'But I would be very happy if you could come and visit me another time.'

Make sure that the note is phrased carefully, otherwise it might put off your friends from visiting you at all.

COOKING WITH A WOK

Preparing food the Chinese way

Always wash your food carefully. Food which you want to eat raw must be washed in boiled water and peeled. Everything else must be cooked thoroughly to destroy germs (see Chapter 10, Staying Healthy).

Heat some oil in the wok, then add chopped vegetables, one after the other, pushing those which are already cooked to the side of the wok where they keep warm. Woks are difficult to clean. They tend to get rusty if touched by water, so you may prefer to just wipe them.

Quick recipes for beginners

In Figs 4 and 5 are two tried and tested recipes for which you will find the ingredients in every part of China, in every season.

Cucumber with coriander

Ingredients for two

2 small cucumbers, 10 stalks of fresh coriander (more if you like), 200g rice, soy sauce, sesame oil, various Chinese herbs and spices, salt, pepper, boiled water

Preparation

Wash the rice three times in plenty of water, each time skimming off any dirt and straw from the surface and picking out bad grains. Put the rice with water into your electric steamer and switch it on.

Wash and scrub the cucumbers, but do not peel them. Cut them into 2cm large cubes. Wash the coriander thoroughly and chop it finely.

Heat five tablespoons of sesame oil in your wok. Stirfry the cucumbers, then the coriander. Add eight tablespoons of soy sauce,and two teaspoons of mixed Chinese spices, as well as a little salt and pepper. Simmer for three minutes.

The correct way of serving this dish is by placing the cucumber on a serving plate and the rice in bowls. However, the dish is delicious if you mix the cucumber, the sauce and rice thoroughly.

Can be kept in tbe fridge and reheated the following day, or frozen.

Fig. 4. Cucumber with coriander.

Di San Xian "Three vegetables"

Ingredients for two

150g rice, 1 large aubergine (eggplant), 2 medium-sized green peppers, 2 large potatoes, 1/2 small onion, salt, pepper, a lot of boiled water, various Chinese dried and powdered herbs and spices (whatever you can buy in your market, but ginger is a must), sunflower oil, soy sauce, a small amount of thickener (eg cornflour) if required and available

Preparation:

Wash the rice three times in plenty of water, each time skimming off any dirt and straw from the surface and picking out bad grains.

Wash the aubergine in boiled water, cut it into 1cm thick slices and chop these into approx 3x3cm large squares. Put into a bowl, salt lightly, cover with a plate. Peel and chop the onion into approx. 1cm large cubes. Wash the peppers and chop them into approx. 3cm large pieces. Wash, scrub and peel the potatoes, cut them into approx. 3cm large cubes.

Cook the rice with water in your electric steamer.

Drain the aubergine pieces (some dark bitter liquid will have accumulated at the bottom of the bowl), squeeze them gently.

Heat eight tablespoons of sunflower oil in your wok. Stirfry the vegetables in the following order: potatoes, aubergine, onion, peppers. Stir continuously, always pushing the already fried vegetables towards the sides of the wok.

Add five tablespoons of soy sauce and two tablespoons of mixed Chinese spices, plus a little salt and pepper and thickener if required. Simmer for a couple of minutes. Serve vegetables on a plate. Serve rice in a bowl.

Fig. 5. Di San Xian ('three vegetables')

5
Living in China

SHOPPING

If at all possible, take a Chinese friend or colleague with you when you go shopping for the first time. Not only will they be able to point out where to get things, but they can also make sure you get a fair price. Students are keen to act as guides and interpreters.

Street markets

Markets are the centre of Chinese life, colourful, lively and picturesque. Here you can buy almost anything: fruit and vegetables, household utensils, shoes, clothes, sun hats, cosmetics, eggs, noodles and pickles. There is more variety of fruit and vegetables in summer than in winter, and more in the south than in the north. In the north, your choice during the winter months can be limited to tomatoes, apples, oranges, bananas and pears which taste slightly 'off'.

Some traders try to overcharge foreigners. If you know what goods should cost, you can reject exorbitant demands. Take a friend with you if necessary.

Department stores

Goods which were unknown five years ago take up a lot of space in the shelves now. You can buy canned soft drinks, household utensils such as baking ovens, hair dryers, buckets and baking tins, a wide range of cosmetics, shoes, clothes, underwear, material, curtains, badminton sets, stationery, pocket calculators, instant coffee, coffee whitener and so on. Department stores in large cities stock some western cosmetics (such as Ponds and Nivea), and tampons.

Prices are marked on the shelves. You either pay the sales staff directly, or you choose your goods at the relevant counter, obtain a coupon, take this to the cashier at the other end of the store, pay, obtain a stamp on the duplicate of the coupon, take it back to the counter, and exchange it for your goods which have been wrapped up in the meantime. This system can be a little complicated, but it creates jobs!

Rice and oil shops

You won't find rice or oil in department stores, street markets or corner shops, but every shopping street has its rice and oil shops. Find someone with a car who can help you transport your goods, and buy a big sack full of rice. It will last. Wholegrain rice is difficult to obtain. Remember to wash rice three times in plenty of water before cooking it, skimming straw and dirt off the surface.

The two main varieties of cooking oil are sesame and sunflower. Sesame is considered the superior oil, and more expensive. Sunflower oil is of a lower quality than that used in the west. You must take your own jar, can or bottle to the shop and have it filled with oil.

Corner shops

You'll find at least one of them on or near your college campus. They sell candles, matches, sweets, detergent, biscuits, basic foodstuffs and some stationery. They also have soft drinks—sweet banana, orange, lemon or peach flavoured lemonades—in bottles or cans. The bottled drinks are cheaper. You drink them on the spot, or pay a deposit for the bottles if you want to take them home.

Street food stalls

Delicious food, local specialities. However, they are not always safe. Don't buy cooked food from street stalls for the first few weeks of your stay, and then only from stalls which are frequented a lot by the Chinese and have a rapid turnover, and where the food is prepared on the spot, or covered.

Some street traders offer doufu, which you can buy in sheets or blocks and cook at home, and which is an excellent source of protein. In the cities, some street stalls sell ice cream and yoghurt. The yoghurt is natural with a little sugar; you drink it on the spot and hand back the bottle or ceramic jar.

Friendship stores

These used to be important sources of western goods, and only foreigners were allowed to use them. Now that they are open to everyone, and that ordinary department stores have included western products in their range, friendship stores are less exciting.

They are mostly frequented by tourists who have little time but a lot of money to spend. There is one in most provincial capitals. If you are in Beijing, and want to buy lots of souvenirs in one place before returning to your home country, visit the biggest of them, in Jiangguomenwai Ave.

Foreign language bookstores

Here you can buy some of the classics at very cheap prices, some textbooks for teaching English, and Chinese-English dictionaries, which are not very good, but remarkably cheap, books with anecdotes in English language, which make nice gifts for your Chinese friends, as well as maps of the world and of China.

What to buy when you visit Beijing

Stock up on goods which you cannot obtain at your placement. The best place to go for the widest range of western cosmetics is the Lufthansa Store in the Lufthansa Centre, near the Sheraton Great Wall and Hilton Hotels.

Stock up on cheese, which is virtually impossible to get anywhere else. Some hotels, including the Friendship Hotel, have shops which sell small bars of cheese, quite expensive by Chinese standards, and not exactly exciting in taste, but an invaluable source of minerals and proteins, especially for vegetarians. If you come to Beijing only once a year or so, consider buying a whole loaf of cheese (about 300 yuan) at the huge friendship store in Jianguomenwai Ave.

Several varieties of bread, including vollkorn bread (10 yuan), dark loaves (5 yuan) and farmer bread (10 yuan), can be bought at the gourmet corner of the Jianguo Hotel in Jianguomenwai Ave. Great if you are tired of the sweet, limp variety of bread you get elsewhere! These loaves keep and freeze well.

The shop in the No. 2 building of the Friendship Hotel sells real orange and grapefruit juice, which is quite expensive but tastes wonderful if all you've had for months are hot water and sugary lemonades. The shop in the No. 1 building sells a wide range of beautiful silks for about 10 yuan per metre.

Beijing's department stores are the places to look out for good material, especially cotton, if you can't get it at your placement.

You will also find better tape recorders, shortwave radios, etc in Beijing than at your placement.

GETTING THINGS DONE

Having your hair cut

Be prepared to cause a sensation if enter a hairdressers' and your hair is blonde or brunette. Ask your friends or colleagues to recommend a good, clean shop. The normal treatment includes a thorough wash, a head and neck massage during which they will scratch your scalp thoroughly with long hard fingernails to remove any remaining dirt or dead cells, a quick rinse, a trim and a blow dry.

Most expats find the services excellent and good value for money. Expect to pay about four yuan in a provincial town, and twenty yuan in a Beijing hotel, for a full treatment.

Having your shoes repaired

Simply go to one of the street stalls, sit down, take off your shoes and hand them to the shoe mender who will repair them there and then. You don't need any language skills, but it is advisable to ask 'Duoshao qian?' (How much is it?) before the job. The work is often done in a somewhat crude, primitive way, so don't take your elegant suede evening pumps.

Having clothes made

Chinese tailors are highly skilled at copying clothes. Many westerners took only one blouse/shirt, skirt, pair of trousers etc with them, and had them copied with excellent results, and at a reasonable price. Working from pictures or patterns did not always work out as well.

The difficulty is, however, to find good materials. Cotton is scarce. For a long time, it was only available on ration coupons, until a campaign was launched to convince the Chinese that cotton was far inferior to synthetics. Today, the Chinese prefer the drip-dry, wonderfully glossy synthetics.

But westerners may feel uncomfortable with nylon clothing

sticking to the sweaty skin in the south, or wearing several layers of acrylics which don't let the skin breathe in the chilly north. The Chinese produce less sweat and body odour, so for them the problem doesn't exist.

Much of the synthetic material is of the sort which has a 'sticky, creepy' feel to it. So when you travel in China, watch out for good material.

Getting your films developed

It is possible to buy print film in most big department stores. However, the quality differs. Chinese makes are not recommended. There are real Kodak and Fuji films, and fakes. The originals come in the appropriate cardboard boxes. The fakes come without boxes, and are of such poor quality that some westerners claim that their cameras were damaged by using the film.

Slide films are difficult to obtain outside Beijing and Shanghai.

You can have films developed in most towns, but the quality varies. There is usually a college or university photographer who betters up his/her income by developing photos. However, if your pictures mean a lot to you, take the films to your home country and get them developed there. Too often, negatives and prints emerge badly scratched from Chinese photo laboratories.

The scope for getting slides developed is small. The Friendship Hotel in Beijing offers such a service with usually good results. Otherwise, take your undeveloped slide film back home.

Everyone wants to have their photo taken with you, and expects to get prints the next day. This is a good way of establishing guanxi. It means, however, that you need two cameras: a good camera with slide or print films which you will probably get developed in your home country, and a small camera using cheap film and local developing services for quick results and next-day gifts.

VISITING THE POST OFFICE

At the post office, you can buy stamps, paper, envelopes and postcards, post your mail and your parcels (not always abroad), and collect parcels for which you've received a notice.

Within China, there is first and second class mail, the former costing several times as much. The post in China can be very slow, so it's worth sending everything first class by airmail. These envelopes are printed in red on white. You must hand them in at the counter to get a confirmation.

Sending a letter can sometimes take an hour or more. The typical procedure is that you take your letter to the post office, buy the appropriate envelope at one counter, go to a table to write the address and sender on it and go to another table to close the flap with glue. Then you join the queue at another counter to have the letter weighed and buy a stamp, take that to the glue table and stick the stamp on. You then take it to a third counter and hand it in return for a receipt.

The glue comes in huge glass jars with big brushes and is a sticky, messy affair. Take your own gluestick whenever you go to the post office.

Second class letters can be put into the letter box. However, it is advisable to ask the clerk for instructions about the latest regulations where to put the address and the sender. Regulations change frequently and differ from one type of letter to another. The author of this book had an urgent letter to her credit card company returned three weeks after handing it in at the post office, because the regulations where to put the address had changed yet again!

Letters abroad require a third type of envelope.

To send a parcel, take the goods to the post office and buy the packaging material there. This can be a cardboard box or a cloth bag. You may be handed a needle and thread to sew your goods into a cloth bag. Jiffy bags are not known. If you take your goods already wrapped up, you will be required to unpack them again.

Not all post offices accept parcels to send abroad (compare the chapter Returning Home).

If you don't receive letters from home, there are two possible reasons for their disappearance:

1. They contained politically sensitive or 'pornographic' material. Censorship exists and spot checks are made.

2. Your friends put a particularly beautiful stamp on the envelope, and a Chinese post clerk, or even someone at your college, has added it to his or her collection.

Case studies

Heather writes from Xingyi: 'I have sent a couple of parcels home by surface mail, they haven't arrived yet. The post office staff aren't particularly efficient. They often get the amount of postage wrong. This happened with one parcel and I had to go there again to make up the amount the next day.'

Joyce and Derek report from Loudi: 'The post office is a continual hassle. They are very bureaucratic and petty in their regulations. Trying to send a parcel is a nightmare. We have to wrap them up in the post office, but without the facilities to do it properly. Mail into China sometimes gets 'lost', Only about eight out of ten issues of magazines to which we have subscribed, like *Guardian Weekly*, arrive.'

AT THE BANK

The best places for changing your money into Chinese currency and for cashing travellers cheques without much bureaucracy are the big hotels in the big cities—such as the Beijing Hotel, the Sheraton Great Wall and the Friendship Hotel in Beijing, as well as the friendship stores.

There used to be only two banking organisations in China, the Bank of China and the 'ordinary' bank. Now there are more, but your best bet is still the Bank of China. You can change your money there, cash travellers cheques, and open a bank account. You are likely to find English-speaking staff there. Branches are in big cities only.

'I have opened a bank account and found it very easy to do so,' reports Heather, an English teacher at Xingyi Teachers College. 'I simply took in some money, and the co-postee's account book and asked for the same.'

Most guidebooks still mention the double currency—one for the Chinese (renminbi), one for tourists (foreign exchange certificate). You could buy certain things in certain shops only with foreign exchange certificates, and the black market flourished.

This no longer applies. Now the only currency is renminbi, with three units: the yuan (colloquially called kuai), the jiao (also called mao) and the fen. 1 yuan = 10 mao = 100 fen.

Credit cards are officially accepted, and many department stores display the Visa, Access and Great Wall logos. In practice, this works well in Beijing and Shanghai. Elsewhere, it can take a whole day for a single transaction.

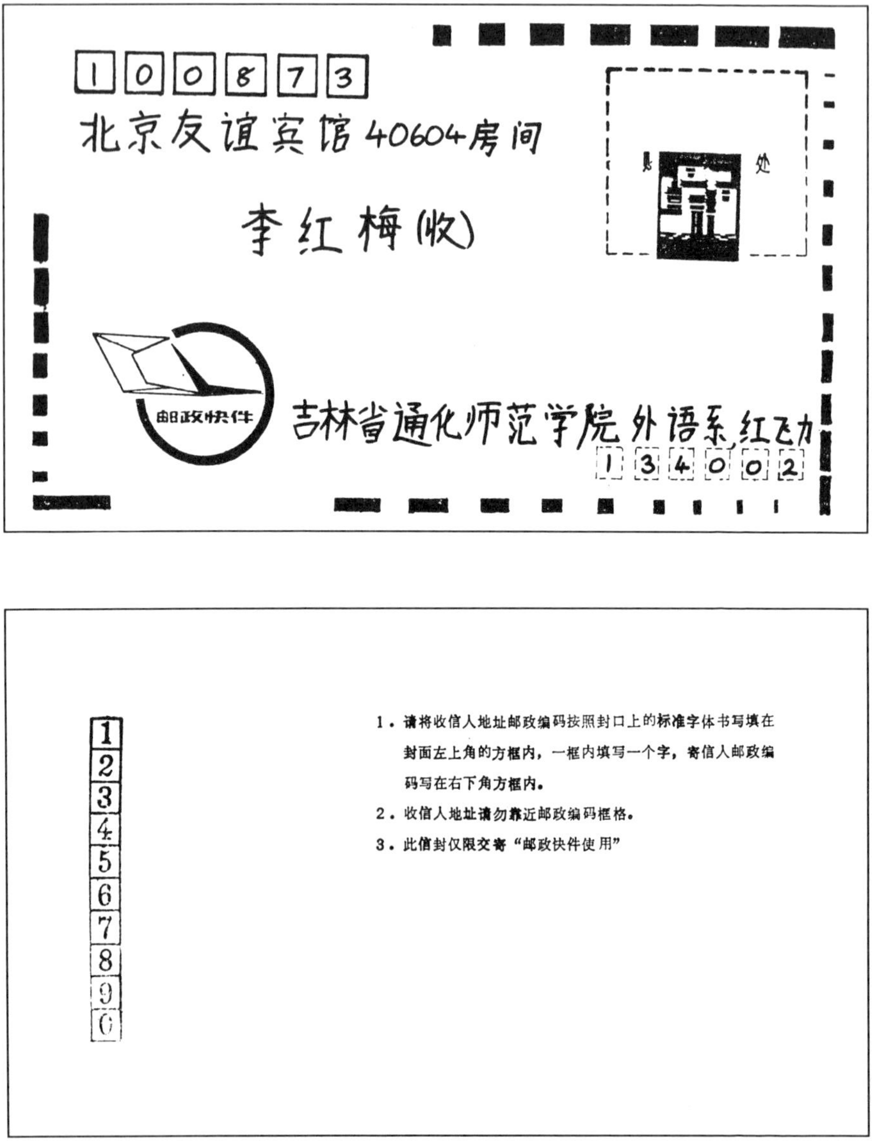

Fig. 6. Correctly addressed envelope for fast mail within China (front and reverse).

Fig. 7. Correctly addressed envelope for international airmail (front and reverse).

Some teachers find that their salaries are not big enough to make it worth while saving with a bank account; others like to put some money aside for travelling.

Fig. 6 shows a correctly addressed envelope, to be mailed within China, for fast delivery. Note that the recipient's address is at the top left, the sender's address at the bottom right.

Fig. 7 shows a correctly addressed envelope, to be mailed abroad, front and back. Note that if there is a single stamp, it is affixed to the top right corner, but if there are several stamps, they go on the back! The Chinese characters at the end of the address mean 'Britain'.

TRAVELLING BY TRAIN

Railway travel: no guanxi? No ticket!

Do you plan to make the most of your stay by travelling from province to province, savouring the flavours of the different cultures? Forget it!

The difficulty is not the huge distances (although China spreads over a similar surface area as the USA), or the available transport (although you may have to hire a tricycle taxi to get to certain places). It is not even that the Chinese don't want you to travel to 'closed' areas (apart from military sites, most places have been opened).

It is just that you will spend more time hunting after a ticket than travelling. Theoretically, you can buy a ticket at a railway station. Practically the railway officials will make it as complicated as possible, for three reasons:

1. The ticketing system is mostly not computerised, and not networked. Every station is allocated only a certain number of tickets for each train, and can consequently sell only a certain number—even if neighbouring stations don't sell any of their allocated tickets.

2. Using, demonstrating and inventing additional complications shows that they are important, powerful people, doing a difficult job.

3. Tickets have a high 'guanxi' value. Railway officials sometimes

give priority to ticket requests from members of their own guanxi network.

So how do you get your ticket? Your employers have probably established a functioning, respectable guanxi network locally and should be able and willing to help. Give them the money and let them buy the ticket for you.

Moving from your first port of call to the next destination is tricky, however. If you want to travel from, say, Tonghua to Meihekou and from there to Beijing, all you can buy in Tonghua is the ticket to Meihekou, whether you plan to stay a few days in Meihekou or just cross the platform to the connecting train.

If it is a matter of changing trains, you can board the train without a ticket and pay the conductor. But you must get onto a specified carriage. This can be number 7, 11 or 14, depending on the route, and it is important to find out beforehand, otherwise you'll be suspected of fare dodging.

But if you leave the station, it can take days until you get a ticket to your next destination, decide in advance how long you plan to stay, and make it your priority from the moment you arrive to investigate how to leave again.

Tickets for foreigners cost much more than for Chinese, because rail travel is subsidised. If you are working in China, you are considered 'Chinese', but you have to prove it by showing your green card. At some remote stations the staff have not heard of the three different categories (Chinese, foreign, green card holders). They will happily charge foreigners and Chinese the basic price, which is fine—so don't confuse them by showing your card.

The problem begins when they have heard (with several years delay), that they are supposed to charge foreigners (that is, everyone with a long nose), a higher price, but have not been told yet that this does not apply to long noses with a green card.

The best idea is to let your employers/friends/guanxi contacts handle the situation and stay well away from the action until you have the ticket in hand.

Class system

There are four categories of railway tickets.

1. *Soft Sleeper* is the most comfortable way to travel. If you are lucky enough to work for a western company in China which

pays you a western salary, you will find it ridiculously cheap. But if you have to survive on a Chinese salary, you won't be able to afford it. Soft sleeper carriages have four bunks to a compartment, with lockable doors, sufficient luggage space, nice clean bedding, a table and a mirror. Your fellow travellers are likely to be male, rich and snoring—businessmen and important officials, polite and sometimes able to converse in English.

2. *Hard Sleeper* is reasonably comfortable and affordable for most. You should certainly consider investing in a hard sleeper supplement if you plan an overnight trip or a journey which lasts more than twelve hours. There are three layers of bunks in an open carriage, and it can be quity noisy, but you'll find the bedding is sufficient and clean. If you have a choice of ticket, try and ask for one in the middle. The top bunks require acrobatic efforts to reach, and are claustropobic with no headroom. You'll have to lie flat all the time! The bottom bunks have ample headroom, but people from other, overcrowded carriages, as well as those from the top bunks want to sit on them during daytime. It can be a problem to find enough space for your luggage. Your companions are likely to be friendly, helpful and considerate, often middle class men and upper or middle class women.

3. *Soft seats* are soft and comfortable for short and medium journeys. For overnight journeys, they are as comfortable or uncomfortable as reclining economy seats in an aircraft. An acceptable solution if money is tight. Travelling companions are often couples, educated, rich and quiet, but unable to speak English.

4. *Hard seats* are an experience, overcrowded, noisy, uncomfortable, smelly, but not to be missed. Great to mingle with workers and peasants. They are open-minded and curious, and will ask you immediately if you are married, how old you are and how much you earn (you can understand and answer those questions in Chinese, can't you?). But, however tight your budget is, avoid hard seats during spring festival and other bank holidays, and for any journey of more than three hours. You may find it difficult to convince a Chinese railway official (or

your guanxi contact who buys your ticket) that you, a foreigner, really want to travel hard seat.

Tips for railway travellers

Whichever class you travel, there will be thermos flasks with hot boiled water, which is safe to drink. Bring your own mug. You can also buy snack meals on the train, or eat in the dining cars. Comments about train meals range from 'Disgusting' to 'Absolutely delightful'. Try for yourself. Most Chinese bring their own food—bread, cucumbers, apples and sunflower seed.

But please, take your litter with you, even if everyone else just drops their paper wrappings, plastic bags and bottles on the floor. One traveller reports: 'At first, I was impressed how the conductresses sweep the floor every hour, effectively removing litter from every corner. But then I saw how they disposed of it: by opening a flap in the wall . . . just throwing it out into the beautiful landscape. I was horrified to see amidst breathtaking scenery, wide strips of red and white litter along the railway tracks.'

The Chinese may not be aware of the long-term effects of such carelessness—but please don't add to the problem. Dispose of your litter in bins at major railway stations, where it will be burnt.

Take a bicycle lock and chain with you, to chain your luggage to the rail. Some Chinese travellers do the same.

Arrive at least fifteen minutes before the train leaves, otherwise you may not be allowed on the platform.

OTHER METHODS OF TRAVELLING

Car

The main roads around Beijing are good, and used by cars, lorries, bicycles, tricycles, horse and oxcarts alike. Traffic is busiest at night, when everyone who's vehicle or licence is not quite in order comes out because the police sleeps! The most important rule seems to be that the most expensive car has priority—a dangerous custom if both drivers believe in the status value of their cars. In mountainous areas, expensive looking cars are sometimes held up and robbed by highwaymen.

Bicycle

The cheapest and healthiest method of travelling—except in the cities where the cyclists are exposed to extreme pollution. More and more Chinese switch from bike to cars, and with the arrogance of a superior class ignore cyclists in the road. On a bike, you are vulnerable and exposed. In cities, cyclists have to pay parking fees if they want to leave their bikes at a public bicycle park. Bicycle menders offer their services everywhere.

Bus
A cheap way of getting about. Like everywhere else in the world, they can be very crowded. The prices are usually the same for Chinese as for foreigners, but prices can be different at different times of the day.

Underground
Beijing underground is modelled on the London underground system, with a Circle Line and a Central Line. Travelling by underground is ridiculously cheap, but can be extremely crowded in peak hours. There can be endless queues at ticket counters (no London-style ticket machines yet), so it is advisable to invest in a monthly travelcard which allows you to go straight through the ticket control.

Taxi
In small towns and in the countryside, a taxi can be anything from a man- or motor-powered tricycle to a horsecart or a car. Agree on the price before you travel. In Beijing, taxis are equipped with meters. Most taxis are yellow, and they come in different categories, with 1.20, 1.40, 1.60, 1.80, 2.00 and 2.20 yuan to the unit. The unit price is written on the outside of the taxi. There is also a minimum charge of 10 yuan. Most taxis are yellow. The cheapest ones (at 1.20 yuan) are the vans, which are not very comfortable, but can transport up to seven passengers, so they are a very cheap way of getting around.

Unfortunately, many Beijing taxi drivers are not honest. If your driver refuses to use the meter, or demands up front payment of more than the basic charge of 10 yuan, you should report him or her, stating the licence or vehicle number. However, this is easier said than done, as the staff at the relevant authorities seldom understand English.

Experience shows that foreigners who speak some Chinese (even if its only 'Ni hao'), are less likely to be cheated.

FINDING THE RIGHT SCHOOL

If you plan to take your family with you to China, bear in mind that lessons are normally conducted in Chinese. While very young children often adapt easily, those who have already started their school education may find it very difficult.

There are a few international schools, especially in Beijing, where lessons are conducted in English or another European language. However, they can be quite expensive, and are frequently booked out a long time in advance. Enquire about vacancies as early as possible, either at the schools listed below or at your embassy in Beijing.

- **ISS Beijing International School**. Curriculum based on national curriculums of the UK, the USA, Australia and Singapore, and taught by qualified teachers from these countries. Accredited by the Western Association of Schools and Colleges. Address: 17 Area 4, An Zen Xi Li, Chaoyang District, Beijing 100029. Tel: (01) 426 1059, 426 4995.

- **Alcanta International School**. All levels from Kindergarten to junior and senior high school, offering Chinese and Canadian high school diplomas. Bi-lingual (Chinese/English) classes, taught by Canadian and Chinese teachers. Address: Rongqui, Shunde, Chuangdong. Tel: (07653) 686338.

- **German School**. Sponsored by the German Embassy. Classes taught in German. No pre-conditions for admission, but German language required. Around 120 students. Kindergarten also available. Address: inside the Holiday Inn Lido Hotel, Jiangtailu, Chaoyang District, Beijing. Tel: (01) 436 1953.

- **International Study Group**. Sponsored by the embassies of Sweden, Norway, Finland and Denmark. Children from Scandinavian countries are given priority. Basic knowledge of English required. About 40 students. Address: Diplomatic residential area in Sanlitun, Block 1, Entrance 3, Apartment 1, Beijing. Tel: (01) 532 2293.

- **Fangcaodi Primary School**. Sponsored by the Beijing

Education Bureau. Children of diplomats and foreign journalists are given priority. Basic knowledge of Chinese required. For those who don't know the language, a special class is put on for six months' intensive training. About 250 students. Address: 1 Ritan Beilu, Chaoyangmenwai, Chaoyang District, Beijing. Tel: (01) 509 4328.

- **Pakistan College of Beijing**. Sponsored by the Pakistan embassy. Basic knowledge of English required. About 300 students. Kindergarten attached. Address: 1 Sanlitun, Dongzhimenwai, Chaoyang district, Beijing. Tel: (01) 532 1905.

- **Lufthansa Centre Kindergarten**. Age range two to six years. Address: 50 Liangmahe, Chaoyang District, Beijing. Tel: (01) 465 2021.

- **International School**. Sponsored by the US, British, Canadian, Australian and New Zealand embassies. There is an entrance exam. A good command of English is required. Around 640 students. Kindergarten attached. Address: Jiangtailu, Chaoyang District, Beijing. Tel: (01) 437 6688, ext. 1242.

6
Making friends

For many people planning to go abroad, the main concern is: 'Will I be lonely? Can I integrate with the community. Is it possible to make easy contact with the locals? Will I find friends?'

Making friends in China is easier than in other countries. You may find that everyone wants to be your friend, guide, and interpreter. Talking to you satisfies their curiosity about the west, and helps them practise their English. It also raises their prestige with family and neighbours.

You will find that most Chinese are very kind at heart, and genuinely want to help you. They understand that you are alone in this country, separated from your family (which, to the Chinese, is a tragic situation), that you don't understand the language, that you must eat unfamiliar food, that you are probably helpless and lonely. They will do everything in their power to help you settle in and feel at home.

Most expatriates are surprised how concerned the Chinese are about their happiness. This is extremely reassuring. Chances are that you will never feel lonely. On the other hand, you may sometimes wish for more privacy, and get tired of their well-meant over-protection.

BREAKING THE ICE

Making contact with the Chinese is easy: give them a wide smile, and they will beam back at you! Greet them with 'Ni hao' (pronounced 'knee how'), and they start a conversation.

The Chinese are curious. Be prepared to answer questions such as 'Where do you come from?', 'How old are you?', 'What job do you do?', 'How much do you earn?', 'Are you married?' and 'Do you have children?'

If possible, learn a little Chinese. If you understand the above questions, and can answer them in the regional language or dialect, everyone will be delighted!

ENTERTAINING VISITORS

If you are expecting visitors, tidy up your flat and clean it. Show photos of your home, family and friends. Keep your guest's cups filled to the brim. If you are offering food or drink, and your guests decline it, offer it again. Chinese tradition demands that guests say 'no' several times before they say 'yes'.

Chinese people are delighted to try western food, but chances are you cannot prepare it because you can't get the necessary ingredients.

If your friends offer to cook for you in your flat, accept the offer. Do the shopping together. You pay for the food, they cook it, and you enjoy the meal together. Most Chinese men and women like cooking.

MEETING CHINESE EXPECTATIONS

The role of a guest

When you are invited to someone's house, take a gift. Fruit is always appropriate. You can also consider bringing drinks, chocolate, or small gifts from your home country, such as postage stamps or a book. Don't be disappointed if your host puts away your gift without even looking at it: the Chinese think it is rude to show enthusiasm or gratitude over a present.

Your hosts may select pieces of food and put them on your plate. If it happens to be something you don't like, accept it with a smile. You don't have to eat it!

It is a good idea to try a little of everything they serve. If you don't enjoy it, leave the bits on your plate. Never empty a serving plate completely. This would indicate that the hosts haven't prepared enough, and would make them lose face. For advice what to do if you are a vegetarian and are invited to a meal, see Chapter 10, Staying Healthy.

If you don't like alcohol, say so firmly, with decisive gestures. If you decline hesitantly, your hosts will think that you are only being polite. It is alright to decline strong alcohol, especially if you are a woman. However, it would not be polite to accept spirits at one person's banquet and reject it at someone else's.

Everyone at a banquet proposes a toast. Have a few suitable words ready, and if your Chinese is not up to it, ask someone at the table to translate. For example, you can thank your hosts for everything they have done for you, or praise the host organisation and its work in general, or say something about international friendship and understanding.

Keeping guanxi sharks at bay

Guanxi plays an important role in Chinese life. You do someone a favour. They will return it on another occasion, or they may get someone who owes them a favour to return it on their behalf.

Most Chinese have built a guanxi network. It works on the principle that the more people are obliged to you for something, the easier it is to obtain favours when you really need them.

Such favours can be of help in obtaining a railway ticket, a permission for business or the services of an electrician. Sometimes, guanxi borders on bribe, especially when money or valuable gifts are involved. Keep clear!

Guanxi services which you, as a foreigner, can offer are:

- teaching English
- practising western conversation
- the prestige of being seen with a foreigner
- western postage stamps.

Guanxi services which you are likely to be offered and can accept are:

- help you obtaining tickets
- help with your shopping and cooking
- interpreting and translating.

Beware if someone offers you a service or a gift which is out of proportion for any favour you have done or are likely to do. It means the person is trying to make you their 'guanxi debtor', and will soon approach you with the request for an enormous favour.

Politely refuse any gifts or services which seem out of proportion to keep guanxi sharks at bay, otherwise you can get into an unpleasant situation when you have to turn down their demands.

Favours frequently asked from foreigners is that they obtain a university scholarship in the west for a daughter, son, niece or nephew—or finance their studies. Make it quite clear that you are not in the position to help; that you don't have that sort of guanxi at home nor possess the money.

TAKING UP A CHINESE HOBBY

Joining the Chinese in their leisure pursuits is a good way of meeting people. They will be pleased that you join in, even if you are an object of curiosity rather than an equal member of the group.

You can learn tai chi or martial arts, calligraphy, folk dancing (which is practised mostly by older people), double fan dancing (in the northeast), you can play badminton or tennis, learn Chinese brush painting, and go to the pictures.

EATING OUT

Eating in a restaurant is cheap by western standards, especially outside the big cities. Judge a restaurant by its cleanliness. Look at the floor (are the spittle and the chicken bones cleared away regularly?) and in the kitchen.

Most restaurants don't have a toilet, but they have a water tap or at least a bowl of water, a cake of soap and a towel. Wash your hands before the meal.

Order one bowl of rice or noodles for each person. Make it clear that you want the rice served with, not after, the meal. Some spicy Chinese dishes are delicious with rice, but prohibitively hot without. The other dishes come on serving plates and are placed in the middle of the table, for everyone to help themselves. One dish per person makes a sufficient meal. For an ordinary meal, you can drink hot water or tea. For a special meal, you order wine or beer, lemonade, and perhaps spirits.

If you are throwing a banquet, go to a restaurant where you know that the food is good and not too expensive. Book the banquet in advance, and get the owner's advice on which and how many dishes to order. It is polite to serve up far more food than your guests can possibly eat.

TALKING ABOUT SENSITIVE SUBJECTS

Ten years ago, Chinese people could be arrested for speaking to a foreigner in the street. Now they are free to talk to you. However, the subjects you can talk about are still limited, because:

- Chinese people may be genuinely offended if you criticise Mao, the government, or anything to do with politics.
- They are worried that someone overhears the conversation and reports it to the party secretary and they get into trouble.
- The person you are talking to may have been sent by a party official to sound out if you are politically safe.

These subjects are safe to talk about:

> food, the weather, landscapes, sights in China, your family, their family, money, wealth, income, careers, non-political literature, hobbies, sports, stamp collecting, holidays and festivals, customs and traditions

Subjects to avoid, at least until you have been in China long enough to develop an instinct for what you can say, when and to whom:

> Chinese politics, human rights, Tibet, sex, boyfriend/girlfriend, violence

LOVE, SEX AND RELATIONSHIPS

In love with a Chinese person

Having a boyfriend or girlfriend is almost synonymous with being engaged. If you enter a relationship with a Chinese, you must decide at a very early stage if you plan to get married.

Chinese people may feel strongly attracted to a particular person, but avoid any involvement if they know that their relationship would have no future.

Before holding hands, they investigate their prospective partner's career and family background. Then they begin 'talking love', which means, they get to know each other better, and discuss possible marriage.

If a man and a woman, who are not married, are seen together without a chaperon, it is assumed that they are 'talking love'. They could be talking about English literature, but neighbours will start speculating about the forthcoming marriage.

A couple can change their mind if after 'talking love' they decide that they are not suited to each other. However, this rarely happens. Most people marry their first boyfriend or girlfriend. If someone 'talks love' more than once or twice, their reputation is ruined.

Getting married to a Chinese national

Many foreigners in China marry Chinese partners. But the amount of red tape to cope with can put your love and endurance to a serious test! Both you and your partner need permission from your work units to get married, and he/she needs to obtain a passport, and permission to leave the country. At each stage, a lot of bureaucracy (and possibly bribes) is involved.

Get in touch with your embassy in Beijing as soon as possible to get advice. Do everything in your power to make your partner's relatives like and trust you. Visualise the difficulties your partner will have living in the west, unaccustomed to nearly everything, without a job, and without the support of family and friends. Of course, you may decide that you will spend the rest of your life in China.

It is worth knowing that a few Chinese are so keen to live in the west that they would do almost everything to achieve this goal. Marriage seems a comparatively easy way, and they make advances to every unmarried foreigner within reach. Be suspicious if a Chinese person starts 'talking love' too soon. However, you will probably look through their efforts before committing yourself.

Casual relationship

A brief affair can ruin a Chinese person's reputation and even their career for the rest of their lives, so think twice before you involve someone.

Prostitution had been eradicated successfully under Mao, and the women were retrained for other, useful careers. For many years, prostitution was virtually non-existent in China. However, with the increase in tourism and foreign business, some women have discovered that selling their services is a much quicker way of getting rich than working in a factory. It cannot be denied that prostitution exists in cities like Beijing and Shanghai.

When Mao declared that the vice, and the accompanying diseases did no longer exist, he also closed the venereal diseases departments in all Chinese hospitals. Doctors cannot recognise and treat venereal diseases in China!

If you have sex in China, bear in mind that your partner may be infected with VD, whether through sexual contacts or from donating blood for which non-disposable needles are used. Protect yourself with condoms which are easily available at department store counters. If you suspect you may have caught VD, get a check-up in Hong Kong.

If you cannot imagine a celibate life for the duration of your stay in China, find a job in a community with many other expatriates, and find your partners among other westerners.

Lesbians and gays

In many ways, China is the ideal country for homosexual couples who want to live and work abroad. The Chinese are used to crowded accommodation, and imagine that anyone living alone must feel terribly lonely. For them, it is only natural that you wish to share your flat and your bedroom with a close friend of the same sex.

The Chinese display a lot of affection and tenderness for friends of the same sex. Men holding hands, and girlfriends cuddling each other in public are a common sight, so you and your partner need not feel as restricted as in many other countries—as long as you don't announce that you are more than close friends.

However, 'coming out', and explaining that you are a homosexual, is not advisable. Chinese may react to homosexuality with incomprehension, disbelief, shock or hostility. They may pretend ignorance to save face for you, the work unit, and themselves. Homosexuality is simply unthinkable, at least in the official view.

7
Working in China

You will find that work attitudes in China differ from those in the west. The image of busy blue ants is correct for peasants and labourers, who often have to work hard, with physically demanding jobs and long hours.

But clerical or teaching staff are relaxed about work. In many offices (especially in big organisations), you will find staff sitting around, drinking innumerable cups of hot water, smoking cigarettes and chatting for five out of six working days. This is normal for them. After all, they have not used all their guanxi and connections, and paid a lot of money to get the appointment, to do hard work!

Every business is equipped with at least one bed for employees to take a xiuxi (break). If it is a business with one room only, then the bed is in that room, between the computer desk and the chairs for visiting clients. Many people make use of the bed during the long lunch break, but in some offices staff take turns to doze peacefully during the work hours.

In schools and colleges, despite the shortage of teachers, there are often teachers who receive a full salary but teach as little as two or four hours a week, or sometimes not at all!

Presence is all that is required, and maybe not even that. Many of the 'teachers' on a college's payroll have another, unofficial job.

For you as a foreigner, this can mean that you are not supposed to do a lot of work either. Workaholics may get frustrated at this attitude. If you are a more laid-back person, you can join the hot-water-and-gossip circle, write your private letters or do crosswords during work hours.

On the other hand, some employers will exploit the foreigner's willingness to the full and get as much as possible for their money. You may find that you are working day and night, coping with a busy and stressful schedule, while your colleagues in the other room are playing Mah-jong, complaining that they are overworked.

Something you will not find in a Chinese office is a coffee machine—but there will always be a supply of hot boiled water in thermos flasks. Buy a Chinese mug for your desk.

CHECKING THE CONTRACT

Make sure that you have a contract, or letter of invitation, from your employer—otherwise you won't be granted a visa. Ask for a detailed job description as well as a written confirmation of everything promised to you.

What the contract must contain

- Your job title.
- A job description: your tasks, responsibilities, who your boss is and who will be working for you.
- The monthly salary, preferably with a clause regarding increases, or linking it to the inflation rate.
- If accommodation is provided. If yes, how many rooms, furnished/unfurnished? Equipped/unequipped? Who pays the bills (electricity, water, gas)—you or the employer?
- Work hours, and number of work days per week.
- Annual leave entitlement.
- Period of stay.
- Conditions of notice.

Job descriptions—and the reality

Be prepared to do work which is very different from what you came to do! If your brief is to teach six hours per week business English to adults at an advanced level, and eight hours conversational English to two classes of first year college students, you may find that you are expected to give music lessons, a course on

British history and a class of technical English for engineers instead.

All this for no apparent reason! While you are struggling with the unfamiliar subjects (you are totally unqualified as a music teacher, your knowledge of technical terms is nil, and you haven't brought any history material with you), you are not allowed to teach the business and conversation students, who had been looking forward to your lessons.

In most cases, the job description differs from reality, although in most cases you will discover a few similarities.

If you enjoy your different job, fine. If not, you can use your written job description to back up your complaint.

Accommodation

In China, it is the employer's responsibility to arrange accommodation for staff and their families. Ask for detailed information of what type of accommodation you will get. This will, naturally, depend on the employer's budget, on the area in which you will be living, and on your status as a foreign expert.

Usually, you can expect a flat with a bedroom and a living room, a kitchen and a bathroom, decorated and furnished. A request for the following equipment will be considered reasonable: fridge, washing machine, shower, television, gas cooker, bicycle. You can try and negotiate for: shortwave radio, tape recorder, oven, wok, tea kettle, electric rice steamer, cooking utensils.

Chinese bills include electricity (expensive), gas, water, and heating. Your employer may pay for some or all of them.

Work hours

The Chinese work from Monday to Saturday, with Sundays free. In some institutions and companies, Saturday afternoon is free as well. As a foreigner, you are in a good position to ask for a five-day week.

The working day begins early (at six, seven or eight) and lasts until five or six. There is a long lunch break (between one and three hours), and sometimes several short breaks.

Annual leave

Some Chinese employers grant no or little annual leave to their staff. Insist on an annual leave clause in your contract—between four and ten weeks—otherwise you will be stressed out, and have no opportunity to travel and explore the country! Some foreigners were given ten or twelve weeks annual leave when they asked for it (before signing the contract).

Checklist

1. Do you have a written letter of invitation from your employer?
2. Do you have a contract?
3. Does the letter, or contract, contain both the job title and a job description?
4. Do you know who your colleagues will be, what their names and positions are, to whom you will be reporting and who will be reporting to you?
5. Does the employer provide the accommodation?
6. If no, is he or she going to help you find suitable lodgings?
7. If yes, how far from the workplace is it situated?
8. How many rooms does it have?
9. Is it furnished? Check for bed, table, desk, cupboard, shelf, wardrobe, chairs, rugs or carpets, curtains.
10. Is it fully equipped? Check for a fridge (if possible with freezer), washing maching, gas cooker, shower, western-style toilet, bathtub (not for bathing, but essential for storing water).
11. Are you, or your employer, paying for electricity, heating, water and gas?
12. Is your employer providing a bicycle for you?

ADAPTING TO THE WORK ENVIRONMENT

Work attitudes

You cannot change your Chinese colleagues' work attitudes, but you may have to change yours. This may, in some cases, mean slowing down your work pace.

Your employer expects you to work more efficiently than your colleagues, which is why he or she is probably paying you more. So by all means, do a good job. But don't boast how fast you are—otherwise your colleagues, who need longer to do the same job, lose face.

If you notice that your colleagues become uneasy when you do in half a day what is supposedly a one-week job, take a xiuxi and have a cup of water!

Relationships with colleagues

Your presence may cause a sensation. Perhaps your colleagues have never seen anyone with blond hair and a large nose before. They will watch you with the curiosity and fear with which you would watch a new colleague just arrived from Mars, with green skin and horns on his head!

Smile a lot to reassure them that, although you come from a different world, you mean no harm!

The experience of working next to a foreigner gives your colleagues a lot to talk about with their neighbours and friends. Knowing a foreigner personally raises their prestige.

Your colleagues will treat you as someone special, like a VIP. Not only has their employer probably asked them to look after you, but they feel responsible for you.

This can be reassuring, especially during the first few weeks in China, when you have not built your own social life and circle of friends. You can ask your colleagues' advice even on matters unrelated to work. They will go out of their way to help you.

The other side of the coin is, of course, that their patronising attitude and constant interference with your private life, can be irritating. Some foreign workers find that they are being treated like a valuable piece of office equipment—permanently on display but hardly ever used in the work process.

Your Chinese colleagues will find it difficult to believe that you actually volunteered to work in China. Most of them dream of living in the wealthy west, and cannot imagine that anyone *wants* to live in China. They think you must have committed a political crime or done some dreadful deed for your government to penalise you and sending you abroad, even if they pretend to believe you.

The most believable explanations are: 'I want to help the Chinese people' and 'I want to learn the Chinese language'.

Always remember that you can probably learn from your colleagues as much as they can learn from you. They are a valuable source of information and understanding. Share your skills with each other.

You and your boss

The relationship between employers and employees resembles nineteenth-century capitalism more than the communist ideal.

The employer has enormous power. For example, if the employer chooses, he can pay only part of the wages to penalise staff he thinks were not working hard enough that month. Some will deduct a substantial chunk from the wages of anyone who has been ill for a day or more.

It is quite normal for staff to fear their boss. The Chinese are not normally allowed to change jobs and find a new employer. They are assigned to a particular work unit and are expected to stay with it for the rest of their lives, unless special circumstances justify an exception. And even then they pay a huge penalty!

You, on the other hand, are a treasured possession the employer does not want to lose—and you are free to leave at any time.

How to deal with difficult situations

When problems arise, be firm, patient and polite. If a situation arises shortly after your arrival which is unacceptable to you, then speak up straight away. You may find it difficult to find the confidence to complain if everything around you is alien, but it is easier to get things changed at the beginning than later on.

You will need a lot of persistence. If something is important to you, bring the matter up again and again.

If your boss treats you in a way which is unacceptable to you, remember that you are in a stronger position than a Chinese employee. Your boss needs you. You can probably find another job in China more easily than he can find another foreigner. Don't hesitate to point that out.

But whatever you do, remain respectful and polite. If you criticise someone, avoid doing it in the presence of others. Never make anyone feel embarrassed. Losing face is the worst which can happen to a Chinese person, and can seriously damage a good working relationship.

Making your boss or colleague lose face can be a powerful weapon. Remember that you possess it, and that you can use it if a situation becomes desperate—but only then.

One Englishwoman worked for a Chinese company for seven months, and still had not seen a yuan of her promised monthly salary. The employer fobbed her off with excuses. When she had no savings left to pay for food, gas and electricity, she reminded him politely of the outstanding salary in the presence of other Chinese business people. The next day she had her money—in cash. He had lost face.

If you have come to China with an organisation or agency, don't hesitate to ask them for advice on how to deal with a delicate situation. Their field staff have probably come across similar situations before and can suggest ways of dealing with them tactfully.

One difficulty which many foreigners encounter is that they are not kept informed about what goes on. An important meeting takes place, and the first you hear of it is when your colleague asks you on the following day why you did not attend.

Your lessons may be cancelled, or extra lessons be added to your schedule, and nobody tells you. You may be told that you have to go on a nine-day business trip now, that the chauffeur will take you to the airport in ten minutes. What, you have not packed your suitcases? Why not?

One reason is that the information is available to everyone—usually on a huge noticeboard in Chinese language.

The second reason is that everyone assumes that everyone, especially the clever foreigner, knows about everything!

Choose one colleague with whom you work closely and with whom you get on well, and ask him or her to tell you about everything, even if they think you know about it already. You may have to repeat your request several times, but after a while it works!

MEETING THEIR EXPECTATIONS

Because the Chinese government invites 'foreign experts', your boss and colleagues expect you to be an 'expert'. Sometimes, this image can put a lot of pressure on a foreigner. You are expected to be perfect.

Have confidence in your skills—you would not have got the job if you didn't have the expertise to do it. At the same time, emphasise that you regard your colleagues as equal experts in their field, that you are happy to share your expert knowledge, but hope to learn from them, too.

MOONLIGHTING

Many Chinese have jobs on the side to earn some extra money, and if you are strapped for cash, you can do the same. Teaching English to private students, doing the occasional translation for a business or having your photo taken for promotional purposes are all possible.

But avoid accepting a job which a Chinese person could do equally well. Unemployment in China is high, and some Chinese depend on small jobs to support dependent elderly or handicapped relatives whose pension isn't enough to keep them alive.

Consider exchanging your services for others instead of selling them. Edit and proofread the English instructions for a new technical product in return for a guided tour of the town. Teach English in the morning in return for help with your shopping and cooking in the evening.

OBTAINING A GREEN CARD

The Green Card is the most important document during your stay in China. Officially, it is your 'foreigner residence permit'. In practice, it is your Chinese passport. Apply for it within the first few days of arrival. Even better, ask your employer or colleagues to obtain it for you from the local authorities. They need your passport and at least two passport-size photographs. The 16-page booklet contains:

Page 1: The document number.
Page 2: Your photograph and signature.
Page 3: Your name in Chinese (ask your colleagues to invent a flattering name which sounds similar to your real name), your name in 'foreign language', your nationality, passport number, date of birth, sex, occupation or status, place of work and

present address (usually the same as the place of work, because in China people don't use private addresses).

Page 3: The name, nationality, sex and date of birth of any accompanying children.

Page 4: The validity and date of issue of the document, and an official seal.

Pages 6 and 7: Room for renewals.

Page 8: Room for changes of occupation.

Page 9: Room for changes of address.

Page 10: Room for changes of passport.

Pages 11 and 12: Room for inspection notes.

Pages 13–15: Room for official 'observations'.

Page 16: Points of attention (how and when to carry the document with you—always!).

Obtaining an Orange Card

The Orange Card is a more obscure document. The booklet with a glossy orange cover is issued by the State Administration of Exchange Control and is meant to be your 'purchasing certificate'.

Followed by your photo, name, passport number and nationality on page one, together with some official looking red seals, are the pages 'Record of Transportation Expenses' 'Record of Accommodation Expenses', 'Purchasing Records' and 'Record of Expenses'—plus an instruction on how to use it (in Chinese).

Theoretically, this document permits you to buy things in China. But all foreigners—residents and tourists alike—are urged to spend their money in China anyway!

You are supposed to have every single purchase you make entered into the book and confirmed by the vendor with signature and seal. In practice, there wouldn't be enough room for them all.

It has been suggested that foreigners can get discounts on showing the Orange Card. But in the author's (and other people's) experience, department store cashiers and railway officials either didn't know what to do with it (which prolonged the process of buying something by several hours), or they *increased* the price!

Another apparent use is to prove how much you have paid for certain goods you are taking out of the country. But none of the people interviewed for this book reported that they had to produce the card at the customs.

Supply the colleague who is obtaining the Green Card for you with a few extra passport-size photograph, and ask him or her to get an Orange Card at the same time. It doesn't do any harm to possess one. But don't use it unless someone asks for it.

CASE STUDIES

Heather has no problems

A VSO English teacher at Xingyi Teachers College, Heather was not told in advance which hours she would be teaching, but she has experienced no problems: 'I only teach in the mornings, two hours a day, except Tuesdays when I teach four hours.'

Sally regrets not having a contract

Teaching at a private school, Sally regrets not having defined a contract with clearly defined work hours: 'I am teaching 37 hours a week—plus preparing lessons, marking papers, writing course material and curriculums. I think I am working about 80 hours a week. Luckily, they've promised me a 10-week holiday. I need it!'

Hendrik Jan has difficulties

'My work has never been what I expected it to be,' says Hendrik Jan, a volunteer with VSO in the Jiangxi Province. He is an entomologist, teaching insect ecology. 'What I'm actually doing resembles the job description, but the circumstances make it sometimes hard to stay motivated. For example the total lack of motivation in the students. They don't seem to realise they're privileged people because they have the chance to study (only 1.4 per cent of the population are studying at a college or university). But I realise they never chose to study at an agricultural university.'

The fact that Chinese students have little say in what they have to study doesn't help. 'Very few students are interested in agriculture, let alone a specialist course in insects, taught in a language they can't understand!'

Another example: 'Only 10 per cent of our students have passed the lowest English test. This is the lowest score of all the schools I've heard of in Jiangxi. This doesn't make it easy to teach a specialist course in English. Even my translator's English is very poor! Another thing that's really bothering me is the lack of co-operation from the officials at my college. Makes you wonder why I'm here. I'm only an object of prestige.'

Christine finds discrepancies between her contract and reality

The author of this book remembers a few discrepancies between contract and reality:

'According to my contract, my flat had two fully furnished rooms with double glazing, a fully equipped kitchen with fridge and washing machine, and a bathroom with running hot and cold water, which had sounded reassuring when I accepted the job.

'I arrived late at night, after a gruelling 30 hours car journey, feeling stiff and frozen, and looking forward to a nice, long, hot bath. But I found the place almost empty, with little furniture. No table, no chairs, nothing—except a huge colour television.

'The window panes were broken, the thin curtains blowing in the icy wind. The outside temperature was around –20 degrees centigrade, and the central heating did not work.

'The fridge was there, but useless, because nobody had thought of connecting the electricity. Not that I needed a fridge, at those temperatures!

'I was touched by the kind gesture of a colleague who had put a bar of soap and a small towel on the sink. But there was no water, hot or cold. Because the flat had been unoccupied for several months, somebody had removed the water pipes and put them to better use . . .

'The contract also specified the equipment I would find in the editorial office; for example, my own computer. Well, I thought. It will probably turn out to be an old mechanical typewriter— They gave me a pencil!

'According to the job description, I was supposed to be the copy editor of the newspaper, with a briefing to improve the contents of the publication, develop ideas, write articles, etc. But I found that I was not supposed to do any work. All that was required was my daily presence in the office and my name and photo in the paper.

'Having a real foreign copy editor gave the newspaper the edge over its competitors. Once a month I was taken on a promotional tour, speaking at conferences to hundreds of people, for many of whom I was the first foreigner they had ever seen or heard.

'My colleagues, whom I found to be very friendly and helpful, thought that I was very lucky being paid for doing nothing. They were amazed that I insisted on getting involved in the editorial work.

'So I spent much of my time sitting idly at the desk, planning the outline for this book, writing private letters and visiting the accountant who enjoyed doing my hair, plaiting it the Chinese way.

'Only gradually did I manage to convince my employer and my colleagues of my desire to work and create an editorial role for myself. "You work too hard and too fast," they kept telling me. "Xiuxi, xiuxi!" (Take a break).'

Sue gets used in rivalry

English teacher Sue experienced a similar situation. 'Everything looked alright in the contract. I was supposed to teach college students conversational English. There were two other American native teachers with similar briefings. But none of us was allowed to teach, or even to go to an English corner or make other contact with students.

'It was clear that the headmaster wanted to keep us out of the way.

'We never found out why they employed us in the first place. After all, they had to pay us a salary which was, by Chinese standards, substantial.

'The only explanation we could come up with was the rivalry between this college and another teachers' college in the neighbouring town. The other college boasted two photocopiers and two foreigners, so our college tried to do even better. They acquired three photocopiers (which were hardly used) and three foreigners.'

Andy has to work long hours

'My work hours were ridiculous,' says Andy, an international trade adviser. 'There wasn't a lot of real work to be done, but I had to be there from very early in the morning until late in the evening, including Saturdays. And on Sundays, which were meant to be our free days, our boss called us in for political meetings. Everyone had to attend. Even me—although I couldn't understand a word of the political lectures.'

8
Teaching English

China invites large numbers of fully and semi-qualified English teachers every year. With a TEFL (Teaching English as a Foreign Language) course behind you, you are well prepared for finding a job . . . but what you've learned on the course has probably not prepared you for what you are going to experience in China!

LOOKING AT CHINA'S LANGUAGE TEACHING HISTORY

Traditionally, education, learning and teaching were deeply respected in China. Today, people are sometimes ashamed to mention that they are teachers.

China suffers from a lack of teachers, especially English teachers at secondary schools. The causes go back to the time of the 'Cultural Revolution', when there was virtually no language training in China. Before and after that time, the foreign language taught was Russian.

Now China has decided that everyone should learn English, but there are not enough people whose knowledge of English is sufficient to enable them to teach.

Zhang Hai Xiang, an English teacher at a middle school in Beijing, is a prime example of the changes. He remembers: 'I was working as a Russian teacher, for which I was qualified. Then, suddenly, English teachers were required. I was sent, at the age of 25, to a college to learn English, and within two years I 'qualified' as an English teacher.'

Zhang has since moved on and improved his English at university, but many 'English teachers' are still unable to speak a simple sentence such as 'Good morning, how are you?'

What happened during the Cultural Revolution

Another problem, which also has its roots in the 'Cultural Revolution' is that teaching is a low prestige job. Small wonder, as during those turbulent years students often beat up and humiliated their teachers in every possible way.

The Chinese government is aware of the problem and actively encourages foreign native English teachers to take up postings in China. Placements at secondary schools are easily available, but more importantly, the government strives to place foreigners at teachers' colleges, where students train to be English teachers.

Teachers are recruited against their will

These students are often at the colleges against their will. They would have preferred to go to university to become translators, interpreters or business people, and most of them are scheming how not to become teachers.

Teachers in China are not well paid. They earn, on average, between 120 and 800 yuan per month—the charwoman who cleans the corridors of the same school earns 50 yuan per day, and, as a true worker, enjoys a better social status.

Students may be bitter about not being admitted to university, but they are highly motivated to learn English.

WORKING AT SCHOOLS, COLLEGES AND UNIVERSITIES

If you have high qualifications (such as an MA degree) and a lot of teaching experience, you are likely to be teaching at a university. With a BA degree, or a TEFL certificate, the most likely work place is a college. If you have little or no qualifications and experience, you may still get a job at a middle school.

The role of the foreign teacher

Foreign teachers are usually hired to teach speaking and listening skills, as well as extensive reading. Grammar, writing and intensive reading are taught by Chinese staff. Students will think themselves fortunate to have a foreign teacher. They will be highly motivated: 'Here is a real westerner!'

As a native English teacher, you may be the only person from whom they can learn English in active use. You are also a cultural source for information about what life is like in other parts of the world.

You and your waiban

The section of your college responsible for foreigners is the Foreign Affairs Office (wai shi ban gong shi), and the person allocated to look after you is your waiban. He or she is responsible for your salary, your accommodation, your health and security, and may be reprimanded if something happens to you.

Waibans can be wonderfully supportive people, eager to sort out any difficulties you may have, representing your interests at the college, organising your travels and generally making your life as pleasant as possible.

Or they can be arrogant and indifferent, promising to 'look into the matters' about which you are complaining, without ever doing a thing.

A third category is the overprotective waiban. They restrict your freedom to move, insist you ask their permission each time you leave the college campus, and force unwanted escorts on you at all times. This type of waiban is also likely to have a key to your flat and to use it—to make sure 'everything is alright' (which includes spying for politically suspicious material).

Try and build a good relationship with your waiban, and demonstrate that you are a sensible, independent person. If you can't get on with them at all, be polite and greet them at all times, but ignore their existence otherwise. Find yourself another mentor at the college.

Fee-paying students

Students who fail the college entrance examination can join certain college courses as fee-payers. In some cases, they can obtain a graduation diploma at the end of the course, but sometimes they cannot. This limits their chances of finding a job.

Some fee-paying students work hard to learn as much as possible, because their parents have invested a lifetime's saving to give them a college education. Others are there by their rich and well-connected grace, with neither talent for nor interest in the subject, holding up the class pace and relying on Daddy to buy them a good job afterwards.

The tendency is for colleges to admit more and more fee-paying students, and indeed to make all students pay the full fee, with only the best candidates getting a grant from the state.

COPING WITH CENSORSHIP AND LIMITED RESOURCES

Large classes, lack of facilities and resources and censorship are difficulties for which your TEFL course has not prepared you.

Spotting the classroom spy

The department appoints a class monitor (banzhang) for each class. This student's task is liaising with the department leadership, as well as organising various things to do with the day-to-day affairs of their class.

The monitor reports to the head of department, in detail, about the foreign teacher's performance, and represents the class with suggestions and requests regarding your teaching. Regard, and treat, the monitor as the officially appointed representative of the class.

In addition, there is usually a representative of The Party, who may act less openly, but reports all your activities to political organs. If you mention any politically sensitive subject, it will be reported to the authorities. If they decide that you plant too many dangerous foreign ideas in your students' heads, you may have to leave China. This happened to a teacher who used John Major's speech on human rights as a classroom text.

Avoiding taboo subjects

You are in China to teach English, not to preach religion or politics. Remember this at all times. If you have a strong mission to spread a particular belief or philosophy, then China is not the right country for you.

Your presence automatically exposes your Chinese students to a completely new world. Through you, they encounter new thoughts and ideas, and widen their horizons. Don't force it.

Of course you can introduce new ideas, but you have to go about it in a subtle way. Otherwise your students will be scared more than interested, and may feel obliged to report you rather than suffer repercussions for having listened to you.

More than one English teacher has been banned from China. Don't let it happen to you.

Subjects to avoid completely are:

- Chinese politics
- Tibet
- drugs
- explicit sex.

Subjects with which you must deal in a sensitive way are:

- politics in other countries
- freedom of the press, freedom of speech, freedom to choose a job, career, and place to live
- sex in connection with marriage, health or crime
- religion
- the supernatural.

These sensitive subjects are usually OK if the teaching material refers to what is happening in other countries. Avoid relating these subjects to China. Some students may try and draw you into discussions relating the subjects to China: 'What do you think is better, communism or capitaliam?' 'Do you think we should have freedom of the press?' 'Is there enough freedom of speech in China?' and so on. Act dumb, and don't take sides.

The students may be truly interested, but they may be probing how far you are prepared to go and then quote every word you say to the head of department, headmaster, party secretary, etc . . . and you are in trouble. If a student shows strong interest, offer additional information about how things are done in the west. This will allow them to form their own opinion, and to compare the situations in and outside China, on their own, without drawing you into a potentially dangerous situation.

When preparing a lesson which involves a sensitive subject, ask your waiban, or head of department, for permission. Explain why you want to use this particular text, and how your students will benefit from it (emphasise the vocabulary and grammar). In most cases, they will allow you to go ahead. Then, if somebody complains, it is their responsibility, not yours.

How to be inventive

What do you do if you have fifteen textbooks for 180 students? Photocopy the exercises? In China, you will have to think twice.

Most colleges and universities are equipped with photocopiers, but toner (and therefore copies) are expensive.

You may have a small allowance for photocopies, probably something like fifty copies per year, but otherwise you, or your students, have to pay.

Your students cannot afford to pay for many copies, but they want something on paper to take away with them after a lesson.

Here are some options:

- Find out about stencilling possibilities at your school. Stencils are blue waxed papers which can be written on with a ballpoint pen or a typewriter. Most foreign teachers find, however, that they are messy, time consuming, and not working and available when needed.

- Try not to waste space on photocopies or stencils. Squeeze as much as possible onto each page, even if you would prefer to keep texts and exercises apart.

- Some colleges have department typists who type your teaching material for you—but check their spelling! They are not usually English graduates, and it may be quicker to type yourself than to correct their work.

- Get one student to write the text on the blackboard before the lesson begins, for all the others to copy into their books

- If you want something written on the blackboard quickly, perhaps during the lesson, get three students to write three parts simultaneously.

A CRASH COURSE IN TEACHING ENGLISH

TEFL courses tend to be geared towards teaching at well-equipped institutions in the western world, with ample resources. Here are some tips on how to teach English in China.

Your major problem will be coping with classes of fifty or sixty students, and as few as two textbooks per class.

Chinese students—their strengths

1. They have an amazing well-trained memory and can learn long texts and huge vocabulary lists by heart.

2. They are able to deal with language in a structured way.

3. Chinese students are usually more disciplined than western students of the same age group. They apply themselves well to acquiring knowledge and skills.

4. They expect learning to be hard, and will stick at a problem area.

5. They are able to make good progress despite a lack of resources.

6. They have a good knowledge of spelling and of complicated grammatical structures.

Chinese students—their weaknesses

1. They memorise vocabulary and grammatical structures without knowing how to use them! They don't develop an instinct for suitable usage.

2. They rely too much on their textbook being right. For them, the textbook is the number one authority on correct English. Unfortunately, the textbooks available in China do not always justify these expectations.

3. Foreign teachers are often amazed to see that the students who can deal with the most complicated grammatical structures have not mastered the basic ones. Chinese students are careless about basic errors and confuse 'he' and 'she', 'is' and 'are', etc.

4. They cannot differentiate long and short vowels. To them, 'ship' and 'sheep' sound the same.

5. They are not able to experiment or take any study initiatives.

6. Typically, the Chinese are afraid of making mistakes. They dare not open their mouths to give an answer to the teacher's question, for fear that it might not be one hundred per cent

right, and they would lost face. This threatens their potential to improve.

7. Most Chinese students find it difficult to speak English, because they have not been taught to.

Teaching speaking skills

Getting the students to open their mouths is the most difficult task of all. They are afraid of losing face in front of the assembled class. Give them a lot of reassurance and praise, and little criticism. During the first few lessons, ask questions which are easy to answer: 'What's your name?' 'How old are you?' 'Do you have a sister?'

Gradually progress to general questions about subjects with which they are familiar: 'How do you get from your home to the college?' 'What do you do in the evenings?'

Then introduce discussion subjects which are interesting to the students. Favourite subjects are:

- Money: how to make it, earn it, invest it. Which jobs earn most money in China/in the west. Which jobs should earn most money.
- Love (minus sex!) Get the students to describe their ideal husband/wife. Bring carefully selected cuttings from magazine agony columns.
- Stamp collecting (the number one hobby among Chinese students).
- Names (they love being given English names, especially names which mean something, Joy, Grace, Victor for example).
- Sports.
- Traditions, customs and holidays.
- Food and cooking.

Teaching listening skills

If you can afford it, buy a tape recorder cum shortwave radio in

Beijing or another large city (they are cheaper in China than in the west), so that you can record the BBC programmes.

Better still, compile at least one tape with radio recordings on different topics while still at home. Another option is to get together with other foreigners in China and read texts which require several speakers.

If you use a tape recorder (assuming either that your school or college has one and you are allowed to use it, or that you have your own), always take some spare batteries into the classroom. Electricity breakdowns are frequent. Have an alternative lesson plan at hand in case the tape recorder breaks down, too.

If you have no tape recorder, you can read texts aloud, or talk naturally. Remember that the best listening exercise for students is to hear your speaking.

Tips

- Give students a purpose for listening and an idea what they are going to hear, perhaps through warm-up actitivites pre-teaching of key vocabulary.

- Make the tasks natural. Choose listening texts to which a native speaker would listen.

- Try and include some non-verbal clues. When speaking, you can use body language. When recording your own texts, use background noise. When playing a radio recording or similar, show pictures.

- When telling stories, do so freely or from notes, instead of reading complete texts. Hesitations and repetitions will make your language more natural, as well as easier to understand, and they will enhance the drama of the situation.

- Make sure your students have understood your instructions before listening.

- If possible, serve the listening in small portions. It is difficult to concentrate on a long spoken foreign language text.

- Never give your students the written text during a listening exercise—they will simply read, which is easier for them.

Sketches and role plays

At first, Chinese students hesitate to use role plays and to improvise. They lack the confidence. But once they've passed the initial barrier, they love role plays.

The first stage could be to make use of their memorisation skills and ask them to act part of a play. Later, you can give them a theme to interpret, and roles. For middle school students, it is a good idea to stick to familiar (Chinese) subjects, such as shopping for food in the street market. College and university students may enjoy acting 'foreign' scenes.

Games

Students love games. There is no better way to get them to forget their inhibitions and talk! However, your Chinese headteacher or head of department may take you to task and complain that you are 'wasting time, playing games instead of teaching'.

Select games which get the students to talk (the primary purpose), but also increase their vocabulary or strengthen their grammar (the official justification).

Try card games (have the students prepare the cards and paint the pictures) and bingo with numbers or words. You can offer small prizes for the winners, such as a few postage stamps or a foreign newspaper.

Songs

There is nothing Chinese students enjoy more than learning a new English song—especially one by the Beatles! Take at least one Beatles tape with you, and write down the texts.

Remembering vocabulary and structures is easy if they come with a catchy tune.

You can use songs for 'cloze exercises'—the lyrics on the handouts have gaps which the students must fill. Or put up true and false statements on the blackboard. By listening, the students must find the answers. You can also use multiple choice questions to test their comprehension.

Why use songs?

1. They are authentic listening material

2. They are a good source of new vocabulary (remember to pre-teach a few key words)

3. They help raise students' awareness of weak forms and word joinings

4. Songs help them to learn pronunciation and to become aware of the differences between American and British pronunciation

5. Songs reinforce structures and grammar learnt earlier

6. You can select songs which relate to a topic about which you have talked during a previous lesson.

Using *Junior English for China*

Traditionally, all learning in China has been teacher-centred. A teacher must never leave the desk. Students must sit still at all times, and stand up when answering a teacher's question. Most of the lessons consist of repetitive grammar and vocabulary drills.

These methods are good to maintain discipline in the classroom, and to get students to memorise vocabulary, but they don't encourage the use of the language.

Gradually, a new student-centred methodology is being introduced, based on the textbooks *Junior English for China* and *Senior English for China*. Student-centred teaching methods leave many Chinese teachers helpless and confused. They prefer the methods by which they were brought up.

If you are teaching at a teachers' college, you may be required to instruct future teachers in student-centred methodology, even if you have no methodology experience whatsoever! Take a methodology book with you, just in case.

English Corners and other activities

Most schools, colleges and universities have regular English Corners, and you will be expected to organise them or to contribute to them. Keep the atmosphere relaxed; the only rule should be that during the English Corner nobody speaks Chinese!

As the only foreigner, you will be besieged by students and members of the general public, with thousands of questions. Remember to reply in simple language: the participants of the English Corner have different levels of English knowledge.

English Corners are great opportunities to meet people and make friends. If you need help of any kind (eg you need someone to help you with the cooking or to interpret for you when you go shopping, or someone to teach you folk dancing and calligraphy) the English Corner is the place to enquire.

Take your photo albums and postcards of your home town to show.

Some foreign teachers are expected to give lectures and talks at their college, usually on 'British (or American) culture'. Don't worry if you don't feel competent. Simply talk about your hobbies!

Examinations

It is likely that you will be required to hold an examination at two days' notice! Be prepared—always have at least an idea or an outline for an examination at hand.

It is a good idea to give lots of oral mini-exams and tests as part of your course. Oral English, speaking and listening skills are not regarded as seriously by your students and teacher colleagues as the 'real' subjects grammar and intensive reading, because they are not part of the examination.

By introducing your own examinations, you can raise the importance of your course and of yourself as a teacher. The announcement that you will examine your students the following week will make them work much harder—a great ploy when they lack concentration.

Marking systems for oral examinations

Tell your students in advance what they will be tested for. Fluency, comprehension, pronunciation?

The ideal marking scheme takes all the following aspects into account, perhaps with a scale from 0 to 5 for each aspect:

- grammar
- vocabulary
- pronunciation
- fluency
- comprehension
- communication

Because Chinese students need a lot of encouragement to increase their confidence in their oral English, try to give marks that are mostly very good, good or satisfactory.

An emergency examination

You may be required to give an oral examination, without previous warning. Be prepared. Make a collection of coloured pictures in advance (photos, cuttings from magazines, old postcards and so on). It is a good idea to start your collection before you go to China.

Eventually you should glue the pictures onto postcard-size pieces of cardboard. You can buy it more cheaply in China and avoid using up part of your luggage allowance on it.

It helps if you build up a wide selection of pictures, so that when you come to use them you can select something relevant to what you've been teaching recently.

Give each candidate three pictures to choose from, and five minutes to think about the picture they have selected (not longer, otherwise they'll prepare a speech and memorise it). Ask them to describe the picture, then prompt them with questions.

CHECKLIST

Have you packed the following:

- About one hundred colourful pictures from magazines on various subjects, about postcard size or similar.
- Some poster-size pictures to decorate the classroom walls and for speaking exercises (especially sights of London, New York, etc, and film posters).
- Books with ideas for teaching oral English (books for teaching written English and grammar are more readily available in China).
- A few lightweight empty packets (match boxes, packet soups, etc) which you can use to play shopping scenes.
- A tape with Beatles songs (and a transcript).
- Newspaper and magazine clippings (choose articles written in simple language).
- A book on language teaching methodology.

- A book on names, their origins and meanings.

RECOMMENDED READING

There are so many books on teaching English as a foreign language available that it is impossible to recommend which are the best for the level and age groups you will be teaching.

As a rule of thumb, however, buy books which help you teach speaking and listening skills, with ideas for role plays and games. You may also want to take a book on how to teach language teaching methodology. Several foreign teachers were surprised to find they had to give a methodology course and were, consequently, unprepared.

Books on grammar are easily and cheaply available in China.

Two books on teaching English in China are worth having: *Living in China* and *English Teaching Handbook for China* (see Further Reading).

CASE STUDIES

Joyce and Derek are left on their own

'We are employed by a teacher training college as English teachers for "oral improvement"', explain Joyce and Derek, who have been posted by VSO as a couple.

'This means almost anything we like as we have no syllabus, and no scheme of work and are left entirely on our own. This is very flattering in one respect, but leaves us feeling on the periphery of the college's affairs. No attempt is made to integrate our work with other colleagues; we are an "add-on", an optional extra.'

They teach eighteen hours a week. 'This would be a light timetable in a UK college, but is very heavy in a place where some staff do only six hours a week. The long lunch break has a siesta time—essential in summer—and afternoon classes can be hard work, getting the students to wake up.'

Derek adds: 'Classrooms are drab, poorly maintained places, with lots of broken windows, very dusty, broken electrics, rows of desks fastened to the floor or old-fashioned tables and benches. Our greatest joy is the students' pleasure in our attention.'

They found that their job description had given too rosy a view of the available resources: 'We've spent quite a bit of money in local photocopying. The typewriter supplied is a lightweight portable producing low quality output. I strongly regret not bringing my word processor. The quality of my handouts is shameful.'

Their advice for everyone who wants to teach in China: 'Go with the tide and set your targets low, so that they are achievable. Expect nothing to go as you planned and you'll often be pleasantly surprised.'

Fiona finds her colleagues frustrating

Currently working in her third teaching job in China, Fiona describes what she finds most difficult: 'Colleagues don't exactly go out of their way to help you unless you ask them. They just forget to tell you things. Another problem is that you never know the standard of your students in advance, so you don't know what books to bring.'

Her most rewarding experience is the progress of her students. 'When you feel that they've made progress, when a lesson goes well, when they enjoy it, that's fantastic.'

Sarah finds her students are interested

A VSO volunteer teacher at a teachers' college in the Jilin Province, Sarah sees herself as a window to the outside world. 'My students are keen to find out how people live, work and think outside China, and they take this information to the villages where they will work. My presence shows the Chinese that there is life out there, life they had not been aware of. China is opening up; they must become aware of other opinions. And of course it is important for them to hear foreigners speak, to see language being used.'

Sarah's brief is to teach spoken English. 'I do this integrated with other skills. I am also introducing *Junior English for China*. The college leaders don't interfere with my lesson plan, so I'm flexible to adapt to my students needs. I do role plays, show videos and teach songs. "When I'm sixty-four" by the Beatles is their favourite.'

9
Doing Business

As China is opening to the west, opportunities for foreign trade develop at an incredible speed. Just have a look inside your handbag, purse or briefcase, and you will probably find a label 'Made in China'.

Foreign investment is welcomed, and joint ventures are positively encouraged by the Chinese government.

The State Statistical Bureau conducted a random survey of over one thousand joint ventures and foreign enterprises, and the results were published in the national press. According to *Beijing Review* and *China Daily*, 81.89 per cent of foreign investors said that China's vast labour force was a main attraction for them. Half of them said they had been attracted by the broad market. Preferential tax policies were also listed as an important factor; many joint ventures and foreign enterprises enjoy tax reduction or exemption from enterprise income tax.

The Chinese economy is changing rapidly, and information which is correct today may be out of date tomorrow. Chinese laws and regulations are complex and change swiftly, sometimes with little or no notice. It is essential that you contact a consultant specialising in Chinese commerce, and a specialist lawyer, before you commit yourself.

LOOKING AT THE MARKET

The average person's spending power in the People's Republic of China is rising rapidly, and so is, after years of deprivation and basic living conditions, the desire for luxury goods. Department stores are constantly extending their ranges to include goods which most Chinese didn't even know existed a few years ago.

Western goods are particularly in demand, as they are regarded as symbols of wealth and status.

The government is lifting its import restrictions. At present, there are only about fifty goods left which are subject to import quotas and require licences, and most of these are electronics and machinery products. Indeed, China plans to phase out quota restrictions on imports by the year 1997.

ENTERING A JOINT VENTURE

For most businesses, a joint venture is ideal. The Chinese partner provides the market knowledge and the skill in overcoming Chinese bureaucracy, and the western business person contribute the ideas, product knowledge, marketing skills and overseas contacts.

Sino-foreign joint ventures account for 77.86 per cent of foreign investments. In the majority of cases, the investment by the Chinese partner is equal, or higher than, that of the overseas investor.

Questions and answers

Q: Whose approval is necessary to set up a joint venture?
A: You need approval from either the central or the provincial government, depending on the total amount of initial investment (central government's approval is necessary for investments of US$30 million and more), the nature of the investment (central government's approval is necessary if large quantities of raw materials are bought from other provinces), and the identity of the Chinese partner (central government's approval is necessary if the partner is a national body).

Q: Which Chinese laws must I take into account?
A: Depending on the nature of the joint venture, the following laws apply: The Law of the People's Republic of China on Sino-Foreign Co-operative Enterprises, the Law of the PRC on Sino-Foreign Equity Joint Ventures, Regulations for the Implementation of the Law of the PRC on Joint Ventures using Chinese and Foreign Investment, as well as the national and local laws and regulations on labour management, accounting procedures, capital contributions, tax, foreign exchange and so on.

Q. What is the duration of a joint venture?
A: The typical duration of a Sino-foreign joint venture is 15–30 years. Shorter terms are possible, but may not be given preferential tax treatment.

Q: I have heard that products must have a specified amount of local content. What does this mean?
A: To qualify as a local product, goods must be manufactured in the PRC. However, there are no clear definitions what 'manufactured' means. Much depends on the discretion and approval of the authorities. For example, some companies import goods as 'raw materials', and define the finishing touches and packaging process, which is done in China, as 'manufacturing'.

Q: Am I allowed to import products from abroad for assembly by a joint venture?
A: Yes, but Chinese raw materials must be given priority. Again, the decision rests with the Chinese authorities at their discretion. However, most joint ventures prefer sourcing locally anyway, to save transport cost and also to save their foreign exchange reserves.

Q: What happens if I don't want to renew the joint venture agreement when it expires?
A: In the case of a co-operative joint venture, the assets are transferred to the Chinese party. In the case of equity joint ventures, the joint venture could go into liquidation.

Q: How do I recruit staff, and what must I take into account?
A: On the whole, joint ventures can decide freely how to recruit staff; for example, from the Chinese partners' existing staff, by advertising, or on job fairs, or by graduate recruitment. Representative offices are still required to use a foreign service unit, such as the Intelltech Corporation or the Foreign Enterprises Service Corporation, but joint ventures can recruit directly.

The Regulations of the PRC on Labour Management in Joint Ventures using Chinese and Foreign Investment deal with all matters relating to recruitment, employment, resignation, dismissal, welfare benefits, labour insurance, discipline and so on. It is no longer necessary to include provisions for 'political study' sessions in contracts, but joint venture staff and workers have the right to set up trade unions, and the trade unions have the right to organise political studies.

Q: How can foreign joint venture partners remit funds back to their country of registration?
A: By means of dividends, which can be remitted without incurring Chinese withholding tax. Some foreign investors recover profits through the royalty payments from the licensing of technology.

CHOOSING A LOCATION

If the major cost factor of your business is production, you should settle in inner China, or the north and west, where labour is cheapest and government subsidies are highest because of the poverty in some areas. On the other hand, if you want to ship goods from Europe to China, or if reliable transport is crucial, or if you need a highly skilled workforce, go for the coastal cities (Guangzhou, Shanghai and so on).

Expensive and prestige goods are often judged by where they were made, especially if there is no standard by which to measure the quality. Chinese people will automatically assume that goods made in a big city are better than those produced in a remote little town.

You can have no better advertisement for your goods than the slogan 'Made in Shanghai'. Of course, production costs in Shanghai are higher than elsewhere, so you should choose this venue only for expensive goods.

OVERCOMING DIFFICULTIES

The major obstacles to overcome if you want to start a business or enter a joint venture are bureaucracy, and poor infrastructure.

Nothing happens quickly in China. if something is important, it has to be done as slowly and carefully as possible, and important decisions are often delayed. You need bags of patience. Whatever you plan to do, begin the preparations as early as possible.

Everyone wants to work for an international company, so it should not be difficult to find employees. Don't be surprised if someone offers you money to employ his son, daughter, nephew or niece. It is quite customary to 'buy' a good job. However, if you have 'sold' the position to someone, they expect to hold the position for good, and it can be difficult to dismiss them. Needless to say, those who 'bought' their jobs are not necessarily those with the best qualifications, skills and motivation.

Generally, it can be difficult to motivate clerical staff. Traditionally, office jobs have been regarded as 'high prestige, little work' jobs. However, the additional prestige of working for an international company, and higher wages are often sufficient to motivate secretaries and administrators. Workers can be motivated by productivity bonuses.

Bear in mind that our Chinese staff may not have the skills you would take for granted in the west. Your new secretary may not have made a single phone call in her life, and tremble with excitement at the sight of a photocopier!

China's telephone network is hopelessly overloaded. It can take a full day to make a local phone call within Beijing! Trying to get through to someone on the phone is a job you should always delegate.

Most stationery and office supplies are easily available within China, although you will have to spend some time sourcing proper typing paper, correction fluid and gluesticks. Toner for photocopiers is a major expense.

Computers, both Chinese and foreign makes, are best bought in Beijing or Shanghai. If you are based in a rural area, and your computer breaks down, it is virtually impossible to get a repair or replacement.

The art of guanxi plays an important role in the business world. Take care to build a good relationship with all your business partners, and with everyone at all the relevant authorities.

It requires tact to see what a recipient would regard as guanxi, and what as a bribe. Expensive gifts can be regarded as bribes and backfire. Invitations to banquets are always alright, and so are gifts of small items of stationery, such as notepads and pens. A bottle of a western liqueur or spirit is usually appropriate. The safest gift is probably a colourful illustrated book of your home country.

You may be approached by an official or business partner with the request to obtain a scholarship for their son or daughter in your country, as part of a guanxi deal. Make it quite clear that you cannot oblige because you don't have the right sort of guanxi in your country.

BUSINESS CARDS

Have several hundred business cards printed on your arrival, with your name and business address in Chinese on one side, and in English on the other. Ask a friend or business associate to transcribe your name into a Chinese one with similar sound or meaning, and make sure they don't play a practical joke on you by giving you a ridiculous name!

Hand out your cards to each and everyone; it is the Chinese custom.

Fig. 8 shows the author's business card. One side is printed in Chinese, the other in English. The number of the mobile phone was added by her publisher, just to impress prospective business partners—she never had a mobile phone in China!

FINDING OUT MORE

For facts, figures and statistics, refer to *China on Business* published by *The Economist* Publications.

You can also contact the commercial section of your embassy in Beijing. The British Embassy, for example, has a commercial library, and issues informative notes on joint ventures in China.

Address: Embassy of the United Kingdom of Great Britain and Northern Ireland, 11 Guanghua Lu, Jianguomenwai, Beijing 100600.

The Chinese Economic Association is an independent, non-profit-making research association of scholars, researchers, students and business executives concerned with China's economic development. It aims to inform the general public about the subject, and publishes useful research on the Chinese economy. The CEA organises seminars, annual conferences and lecture tours to China. Members receive a quarterly newsletter.

The annual membership fee is £8 for individuals, £5 for students, £25 for non-commercial corporate, and £50 for corporate membership.

Address: Ms Jacky Jennings, Secretary, CEA, R432, STICERD, London School of Economics, Houghton Street, London WC2A 2AE. Tel: (0171) 955 6691. Fax: (0171) 242 2357.

The China–Britain Trade Group offers its members workshops, meetings with Chinese delegations, an excellent informative

ENGLISH COACHING PAPER OFFICE

Christine Hall
Copy Editor

ADD: No.151 Shiyuan Road, Tonghua City, Jilin P.R.C.
Tel: (0435) 619748 616002-2169 Telex: 0049
Fax: (0435)619748 Postcode: 134002
Mobile Tel: (0435)905048

英 語 輔 導 報 社

克里斯廷·霍尔 专职编审

地址: 中國·吉林通化市師院路151號 郵編: 134002
電話: (0435) 619748 616002-2169 電挂: 0049
傳真: (04535) 619748 大哥大: (0435) 905048

Fig. 8. The author's business card (front and reverse).

newsletter called *China–Britain Trade Review* and access to databases and libraries.

In addition, members have up to five days' free use of offices in Beijing, Shanghai or Guangzhu, as a base to work from or to receive visitors. These offices are staffed with bilingual employees who are familiar with Chinese and western work practices. In addition, the offices can obtain market information, arrange meetings for your China visit, pass messages and chase replies, act as a postbox, make travel arrangements, and arrange translation and interpreting services.

Membership costs £1,057.50 including VAT per year. Non-members can use the Chinese offices for £150 per day, and use the London library for £20 a time.

Address: China—Britain Trade Group, 5th Floor, Abford

House, 15 Wilton Road, London SW1V 1LT. Tel: (0171) 828 5176. Fax: (0171) 630 5780.

The Chinese Legal Practitioners Group which belongs to the School of Oriental and African Studies (SOAS), was established in the mid-1980s as a forum for discussing developments in Chinese law. It meets six times a year at the SOAS. Leading practitioners and other experts present papers on recent changes in commercial law and related matters. Individual subscriptions are £25 per year, corporate subscriptions, which also entitle the subscriber to use the SOAS library, cost £225.

Address: School of Oriental and African Studies, Department of Law, University of London, Thronhaugh Street, Russell Square, London WC1H 0XG. Tel: (0171) 637 2388. Fax: (0171) 436 3844.

Other useful addresses:

Chinese Chamber of Commerce, 20 Frith Street, London WC2. Tel: (0171) 734 6502.

Gallup Market Research, G-202, POB 9788, Asian Games Village, Beijing 100101. Tel: (01) 491 1293. Fax: (01) 499 1749.

ACMR Market Research, 3 Yuetan Beijie, Beijing 100037. Tel: (01) 8336084 (information consultancy), (01) 833 6085 (market research), (01) 835 4718 (data services.

Office Equipment Company, Beijing Kangde Group Co., Room 101-102, 47 Chongnei Dajie, Chongwen District, Beijing 1005. Tel: (01) 204 2959. Fax: (01) 203 3364.

The China Europe Management Institute Shanghai, Shanghai Jiaotong University, Minhang Campus, 800 Dongchuanlu, 200240 Shanghai. Tel: (021) 435 9365. Fax: (021) 435 8928.

TRADING WITH TAIWAN

Taiwan's major export items are machinery and electrical equipment, textile products, basic metals, plastics and rubber, footwear and accessories, transportation equipment, toys and sports requisites, precision instruments including clocks and musical instruments, animals and animal products, and chemicals.

Export items with the highest growth rate are information and communication products, iron and steel, chemicals, clocks and watches.

The conditions of business in or with Taiwan differ naturally from those for the PRC. Advice is available from:

Majestic Trading Co Ltd, Taiwan Trade & Investment Service, 2nd Floor, 70 Piccadilly, London W1V 9HH. Tel: (0171) 629 1516. Fax: (0171) 499 8730.

Taiwan Trade Centre, 3rd Floor, 29 Wilson Street, London EC2M 2SJ. Tel: (0171) 638 4982. Fax: (0171) 638 4686.

10
Staying Healthy

LOOKING AT CHINA'S MEDICAL HISTORY

China has an extremely wide variety of standards of medical care. Hospitals can be modern, well equipped, and scrupulously clean, especially some of the hospitals located in the big cities such as Beijing, Shanghai and Guangzhou. On the other hand, you may find hospitals appallingly dirty—so dirty that you will attempt to run away to protect yourself from the most horrible diseases! Investigate local medical facilities before you need them.

The rural areas of China are probably among the most primitive on earth. Due to lack of good health education and preventative medicine, such as immunisations, children still die of tetanus.

Although traditional medicine in China has been practised continuously over the centuries, the knowledge of herbalism is not as thorough and widespread as westerners believe.

The introduction of western medicine into China has been patchy. Many doctors prescribe western medicine without knowing how it works.

The Cultural Revolution—and the consequences

At the time of the 'Liberation', there were very few medical facilities in China, apart from herbalists, and a handful of hospitals practising western medicine in treaty ports. The communist government wanted to extend western medical care over the country, and opened an incredible number of new hospitals. However, there were not enough doctors and nurses to staff them.

The training period for doctors was reduced to three years during the 'Great Leap Forward'. When the 'Cultural Revolution' began, hospitals were already poorly staffed, with doctors who had only basic medical knowledge. The only good doctors at the time were those who had had missionary training before the war.

In 1965, the administration of hospitals was taken over by the 'Red Guards'. Any person with in depth medical knowledge was an intellectual, and therefore bourgeois and suspect. Virtually every good doctor was sent to do manual labour in the countryside. Senior doctors with responsible positions in the hospitals sometimes faced a fate far worse; many did not survive. Training and studying were not encouraged and all medical colleges were closed for five years.

Some of them re-opened around 1972, but offered only part time studies in basic medical care—similar to a first aid course.

In 1978, a real programme was launched to open medical colleges, but there were not enough teachers to train the aspiring doctors. There had been few good doctors before the Cultural Revolution, and some of the best doctors had not survived. Those who had, were rushed to become professors of medicine.

A western medical expert resident in China commented: 'If you find a doctor over the age of seventy, he or she is probably good. A doctor over sixty is possibly good. Doctors in the age group between thirty-five and sixty are very badly trained. Those under thirty-five had the best training China could offer, which was not a lot. And if there is a young Chinese doctor who is really good, then he or she is in America!'

ENVIRONMENTAL POLLUTION

All the big cities and industrial towns in China suffer from pollution to an extent which is worrying—both for nature and for people's health. Some of the pollution is easily noticeable, such as the air pollution from coal-burning for domestic use and for fuelling power stations and industry.

Others are less obvious, but equally problematic, such as the sulphur and chlorine levels in the atmosphere. In many districts, the water is polluted, especially in the very rural areas and the new industrial zones, where toxic chemicals leak into the groundwater and nobody seems to worry about it.

Chinese as well as expats suffer from minor health problems due to pollution: catarrhal colds, itchy eyes and ear infections. If you tend to suffer from asthma, avoid living in China's industrial zones. Apart from this, it is advisable to get into the fresh air of the countryside as often as possible.

STORING AND PREPARING FOOD

- For drinking, use only water that has been boiled. Three minutes of a rolling boil will destroy all germs. Always keep a thermos flask full of boiled water. (Remember to use boiled water for brushing your teeth.)

- Bananas and citrus fruit are safe to eat. All other fruit must be washed with boiled water *and* peeled

- Salads often carry worms and diseases. It is best not to eat any raw vegetables or salads at all (they are all grown on nightsoil from latrines), especially during the first few months of your stay. Avoid salads in restaurants. At home, you can prepare salads by washing the vegetables thoroughly in boiled water and peeling them, but there is still a risk.

- Cook everything thoroughly for at least ten minutes. If this is not possible (eg for salads), you can soak fruits or vegetables in a chlorine or iodine solution, which destroys many germs, but is not 100 per cent effective.

- Keep three separate areas in your fridge: one for raw unwashed produce, one for raw but washed and disinfected produce, and one for cooked food.

- Shellfish tend to live near sewer outfalls and carry diseases. Don't eat them unless you know for sure that they have been cooked in hot water or oil for at least ten minutes. In the interest of your health, politely refuse raw shellfish, however appetising it looks.

- Especially in the north of China, it is difficult (but not impossible) to maintain a diet with sufficient mineral content. Good sources of calcium and iron are celery, coriander, amaranth, vine spinach, short cabbage and mustard greens. Include them in your recipes wherever possible.

Eating out

- Every restaurant has a washbasin or washbowl filled with water. The Chinese don't usually wash their hands after going to the loo, but they wash them before eating. Wash your hands—if necessary, ask for a fresh supply of water—but don't use the communal towel.

- Food is often served in cracked bowls and cups and with used chopsticks which have been washed in a contaminated river. Pour away any water from your bowls and cups. Rinse them with tea which is a mild antiseptic. You can pour the tea on the restaurant floor. Even the more health and hygiene conscious Chinese follow this custom. Then wipe the crockery with a tissue before filling them with food. The bigger restaurants offer disposable chopsticks, but it is advisable to carry your own with you when travelling.

Being a vegetarian

It is possible to maintain a vegetarian diet almost everywhere in China. Without doubt, it is easiest in southern China with its abundance of fruit and vegetables. Inner Mongolia is probably the least suitable place for a vegetarian—the choice of foodstuff is limited, and you will be served mutton wherever you go.

The Chinese don't like dairy products. They find cheese disgusting and regard milk powder as something for little children. Yoghurt is becoming popular in the cities only. Without dairy products, it is difficult for a vegetarian to maintain a balanced diet, because there isn't enough protein. Each person should eat at least four or five eggs per day. Other good sources of protein are beans, peanuts and doufu. Doufu, made from soybeans, is a healthy and versatile ingredient, but supplies can sometimes be erratic.

The Chinese find it difficult to understand the concept of vegetarianism. If you want to give a reason they understand, explain that either your religion or your doctor forbids you to eat meat.

However, the Chinese appreciate that we foreigners eat different types of food, and are glad to know what we like and what we don't. It is important to tell your hosts well in advance. Then they will be happy to arrange a meal exclusively, or mostly, with vegetable dishes. If you tell them of your vegetarianism only during the banquet, and refuse the expensive meat they've already bought and prepared, they will be hurt. It would also be insulting if you accepted meat at one host's banquet but not at the other's.

Layla, a Trust Fund volunteer teacher, reports that the principle of vegetarianism was not always understood by her hosts: 'As food is such an integral and important part of life in China, I would recommend that anyone who goes there should be willing to eat anything put in front of them (especially in the Guangdong Province). It may have been a little different as where I was, was so poor that had I declined the expensive meat it would have been the ultimate insult. As a result. I ended up eating dog, cat, rat, sea-slug, chicken's head and feet, snake racoon, octopus head, cow's ears, pigs intestines . . . all as disgusting as a piece of rump steak to a vegetarian like me.

'They also don't understand the concept of vegetarianism, so those who are have to be prepared to encounter the odd bit of flesh. We were lucky, we cooked for ourselves in our flat, so the unidentifiable creatures only came out on special occasions!'

Some westerners compromise by eating meat in response to hospitality, but maintaining a vegetarian lifestyle otherwise.

PREVENTING ILLNESS

Most expatriates, in any country, find that during the first year of their stay they are ill more often than usual, for several reasons:

- The body has become immune to the bugs in food, drinking water and air in the home country, but not yet to those in the new environment.
- It takes a while to get adjusted to the new climate.
- Settling into a new environment is always stressful, and stress weakens the body's power of resistance.
- Simple house remedies for curing minor ailments, always at hand at home, are not available in the new country, and it takes months to find out about the local alternatives.
- Not knowing the healthcare system, the medicines and the language, many people delay seeing a doctor in the foreign country until the illness becomes serious.
- Expatriate workers try to impress their local colleagues with

their strength and stamina and return to work too soon after an illness, before they have fully recovered—only to become ill again, more seriously this time!

In China, the following aspects can put your health at risk:

- Extremely low standards of hygiene in many eating places, especially in rural areas.
- Extremely low standards of hygiene in public toilets.
- Low standards of hygiene in many hospitals.
- Use of non-disposable equipment.
- Problems with blood transfusion.
- Specific diseases which are not found in western countries (and some which rarely exist outside China).
- Environmental pollution of all kinds (especially air pollution, caused by rapid industrial development).

How to stay healthy

- Be aware of the lower hygiene standards at all times, and act accordingly to protect yourself.
- Eat well. Pay even more attention to a healthy diet than you would at home.
- Keep physically fit. Your body needs more strength than usual to stay healthy or to overcome illness. Tennis, badminton, folk dance, tai chi are just a few ideas for sports and exercises which you can take up and practise in China.
- Take vitamin supplements.
- Keep all your vaccinations up to date.
- Take your malaria medication regularly (if you live in a malaria area).

Recommended vaccinations

Forget about the wall charts in your doctor's surgery. You are not a tourist travelling in well developed areas. You are going to live in China, perhaps in rural areas and under difficult hygienic circumstances, constantly exposed to infections. You should take as many vaccinations as possible. The following are currently recommended:

- Polio
- Tuberculosis
- Tetanus
- Typhoid
- Hepatitis A
- Hepatitis B
- Rabies
- Japanese Encephalitis

Some of the vaccinations are free, for others you have to pay. If you work for a western employer or organisation, they may pay for your vaccinations. Remember that some vaccinations need several courses, with several weeks between them, so start early.

Tests required

It is important to have a blood grouping done before you go to China, as well as an Aids test—otherwise you may be forced to have one done in China, by doctors who use the same needles for all their patients.

Blood transfusion

Certain blood groups, common in the west, are rare in China, and there may be no blood reserves available in the case of an emergency. This includes blood group O and all rhesus negative blood. So if you have group O rhesus negative blood, it is almost impossible to get a blood transfusion.

Worse still, in an emergency your blood may not be identified correctly, because the rhesus negative factor is almost unknown. Rhesus negative patients may be given rhesus positive blood, with disastrous results.

As in all Third World countries, there is the risk of blood preserves and blood products being contaminated. They may carry malaria, venereal disease, HIV, and hepatitis.

What's more, China is almost alone in not allowing the World Health Organisation to look into the country's blood transfusion system, so there is no saying how safe or dangerous blood transfusions are.

Chinese doctors tend to order blood transfusions frequently, even when they are, in western opinion, not strictly necessary. In view of the risks, avoid having a blood transfusion if at all possible, or delay it until you reach a state-of-the-art hospital, or Hong Kong. Naturally, in an emergency, you may not be in a position to discuss the merits and risks! However, you should discuss the subject with your family or other expats beforehand and make sure you know each other's blood groupings.

First aid kit

Your first aid kit should contain:

1. *Wound dressings*: a small selection of plasters (you can buy additional plasters in China), non-adherent dressings, wound dressings, crepe bandage, two triangular bandages, sterile dressings and bandages.

2. *Other first aid items*: alcohol/antiseptic wipes, safety pins, lancets, cotton wool, tweezers, scissors, several syringes in different sizes, at least 50 needles in different sizes.

3. *Medicines*: antiseptic cream, antifungal cream (for vaginal thrush and athletes foot), a small supply of antibiotics (you can obtain additional antibiotics in China), cold remedies which you know help you (you can buy effective traditional Chinese cold remedies), painkillers (available in China, but you don't want to run up and down the streets to find a pharmacy when your first headache strikes you), antihistamine tablets (in case of allergies), antimalarial tablets for the length of your stay, travel sickness tablets, anti-worm remedies, any medicines you think you may need.

There are handy first aid travel bags available, which contain all the necessary items for (1) and (2), including a booklet on how to administer first aid. They only contain about ten needles in two sizes. You need far more, because many medicines are given via injection into your bum, usually in courses of six injections.

Preventing, recognising and treating illness

Diarrhoea

The most frequently discussed topic among expats in China is the state of their bowels! Almost everyone suffers several attacks of diarrhoea during their stay, especially during the first few weeks. The best prevention is to boil all your drinking water and to cook your food thoroughly. As, on average, vegetarians have fewer problems with diarrhoea, you may want to reduce your meat consumption while in China.

Diarrhoea is seldom dangerous. Severe attacks are usually over within two or three days, milder attacks can last longer.

Nevertheless, it robs your body of salt, sugar, minerals and fluid.

Treatment: Add eight level teaspoonfuls of sugar, half a teaspoonful of salt, half a teaspoonful of baking soda/sodium bicarbonate (if available), some citrus fruit juice or coconut water (if available) to one litre of clean, thoroughly boiled water, and drink as much of it as you can!

Typhoid

This illness still exists in rural China, to the same extent as it existed in rural England in the last century. Migrant peasants moving to the towns and cities searching for work carry the disease with them and spread it there. Typhoid is also spread by food or water supplies which can be contaminated by sewage, flies or by faulty personal hygiene. The risk is greatest in areas with poor hygiene standards.

Symptoms include fever, headache, diarrhoea (often bloody), abdominal pain, rash, persistent weakness and constipation, and can be fatal if not treated. Typhoid can be prevented by vaccination which gives 80 per cent protection.

Hepatitis

There are several types of hepatitis, all found in China. The most frequent are hepatitis A, which is carried on infected food, and hepatitis B, which is sexually transmitted and can also be carried on contaminated surgical equipment such as syringes or needles.

The illness results in acute inflammation of the liver. Symptoms develop in three stages:

1. Fever, chills, fatigue, weakness, headache, aches and pains.

2. Loss of appetite, nausea, vomiting, right upper abdominal pain.
3. Light-coloured faeces, dark urine, jaundice of the skin or the whites of the eyes.

Hepatitis may lead to liver failure and the patient may lapse into a coma. Symptoms vary, but if you observe jaundice combined with one or several of the other symptoms, obtain a check-up at a modern hospital at once.

To prevent hepatitis, improve the sanitary hygiene of your daily environment to the best of your abilities. For hepatitis A and B, vaccination is available. Some GPs offer only hepatitis A immunisation, but you should insist on having the hepatitis B vaccination also, because you may contract hepatitis B as a patient in a Chinese hospital where re-used needles carry the infection.

Worms

Worm cysts can be picked up easily from infected food, especially salads. Symptoms are stomach discomfort, loss of appetite, itching around the anus, and bloating. Some types of worms can be seen moving in the stool.

Local hospitals can detect worm cysts in stool samples and prescribe treatment. However, you may prefer to take a worm remedy with you. Worm infections are unpleasant but not dangerous.

Venereal diseases and Aids

When prostitution was effectively abolished under Mao, and prostitutes trained for other jobs, venereal diseases became less frequent. The Chinese government went as far as declaring venereal diseases totally eradicated in the 1980s.

Because the existence of those illnesses was denied, the doctors were not trained to recognise and treat them. Hospital departments specialising in the treatment of this sort of disease were closed.

However, VD still exists in China, and is on the increase again, especially as prostitution is becoming evident in the cities. Aids, too, is spreading.

Condoms are widely available. Use them to prevent sexually transmitted diseases. If you suspect that you are infected, go to Hong Kong or a western country where it can be recognised and treated properly.

Cholera

Officially, Cholera has been eradicated in China, but travellers have reported local outbreaks. There is no effective vaccine against cholera, because the cholera vibrio has undergone mutation and has become immune.

Luckily, the modern cholera is different to the cholera prevalent in previous centuries, and far less dangerous. It is spread by contaminated food (especially shellfish) and water. The main symptoms are diarrhoea, dehydration and vomiting. Treatment is with antibiotics. Self-treatment in case of suspected cholera is the same as for ordinary diarrhoea.

Malaria

This illness is carried by mosquitos. No vaccination is available. In some areas of China, malaria risk exists only during certain months, in some all the time, in some not at all.

Prevention: Due to lack of funds, there is no comprehensive public health programme for mosquito eradication in China. Mosquitos breed in stagnant waters. Identify their living quarters and if possible, destroy them.

Malarial mosquitos are most active at dawn and dusk, so take particular care at these times. Cover ankles and wrists, wear light-coloured clothing, and use mosquito nets. Effective anti- mosquito skin sprays and creams are available. You can also spray your bedroom ceiling, lampshades and curtains with a permethrin spray, then close the door for twenty minutes before you enter the room again.

Several varieties of preventive tablets are available. Which tablets you should take depends on when and where you are going, because some forms of malaria in some regions have become resistant to preventive drugs. Expatriates in China who have taken preventive medication are far less likely to contract malaria, so don't forget your daily tablet. However, some malaria prevention tablets can cause unwanted side effects, especially if taken over several years.

Travel sickness

Remedies for travel sickness can be bought in China, but they are not as widely available as in the west. Most Chinese people travel only once a year, to visit their parents or spouses who live in another part of the country, so there is less need for travel sickness remedies.

Some of the available products have unwanted side effects, for example, they stop you from sleeping for twenty-four hours. If you expect to travel a lot in China, bring a sufficient supply of your own travel sickness tablets.

You can also try the traditional Chinese method: peel an orange, hold the peel under your nose and breathe in the fragrance. It helps for some.

What to do if you are ill

Take any illness seriously, at the first symptoms. Stay at home, rest.

One western medical expert in China warned: 'Always assume the worst. If you feel a tickle in your throat, assume that it is going to develop into pneumonia. In your home country, it wouldn't, but it may in China, unless it's treated properly. Keep a supply of antibiotics. Take a full course if the symptoms don't disappear within three days. I recommend antibiotics only in cases of serious illness in the west, but this is China! We have to prevent minor ailments developing into serious illnesses which cannot be treated properly out here.'

Always take an interpreter (friend, colleague, student) with you to the doctor or the pharmacy. Your employer is expected to pay the doctor's fees. If you know what's wrong with your body, the best course is to describe the symptoms to the local pharmacist. You will probably get more appropriate remedies there. On the other hand, if you want a course of antibiotics, go to the doctor. Always take your needles with you; the doctor may decide to start a course of injections there and then. Tell the doctor if you have an allergy to penicillin.

If things get worse, and if you have checked out that the local hospital is a good one, you can go there. Most of them take outpatients only. You have to buy a coupon at the reception, and give it to the doctor. Extra coupons are needed for X-rays etc. Coupons cost 8 yuan for Chinese and for foreigners working in China; foreign tourists pay a higher rate.

If you believe that you are seriously ill, don't waste any time at local hospitals. Make your way to Hong Kong if you live in the south; if you live in Inner Mongolia, travel into the area of the

Russian Federation, where you will find clean hospitals and well-trained medical staff.

Another option is to go to the Sino-German Policlinic in Beijing. This clinic is fully equipped for both western and traditional Chinese treatments, spotlessly clean, with doctors on call day and night, with a dental and a gynaecological department. The address: Basement, Landmark Tower B-1, 8 North Dongsan Huan Rd, Beijing 100026. Tel: (01) 501 1983. In an emergency, explain to your taxi driver that it is opposite the Great Wall Sheraton Hotel.

BEING PREGNANT IN CHINA

If you are pregnant, or plan to start a family, the best advice you can get is *not* to go to China. Some couples with rosy images of natural childbirth aided by herbal medicines who decided to have their child in China regretted it bitterly. Western medical experts urge expectant women to return home because:

- Resistance to malaria may fall during pregnancy. No anti-malarial regime is fully safe and effective in pregnancy. The rate of miscarriage and still-birth increases if the mother is infected with malaria. Malaria prevention and treatment can have dangerous side effects in pregnant women. (If you have to go to China while pregnant, obtain Proguanil and Chloroquine for prevention and Quinine for treatment, which are considered the safest during pregnancy.)

- Group O rhesus negative blood, the universal donor group, always on hand in western maternity units, is unlikely to be available for childbirth.

- The Chinese have less respect for the life of an unborn child. For Chinese women, who have already had their allowance of one or two children, terminations are often enforced. There is an unofficial eugenics policy. What most couples want, is a healthy boy. This is not official government policy, of course, but couples or doctors seem to come to arrangements. For example, far more boys than girls are born!

  In consequence, doctors are quick with recommendations for an abortion. Any infection the woman or child may have, any minor disfigurement which could be corrected surgically in the west, such as a club foot, or even just because they don't hear the tiny heart beat, is a reason for an abortion.

A woman, who is urged by a doctor to have an abortion there and then, paralysed by the sudden shock, will usually agree. Never agree to an abortion before you have obtained an independent opinion of a western doctor. If possible, arrange for a flight home, or to Hong Kong.

- The hygienic conditions in many hospitals are not such as you would wish for childbirth.

- Chinese laboratories confuse in fifty per cent of all cases the existence of antigens (which mean that the patient is infected) and antibodies (which are caused by the vaccine and act to prevent infection). Nobody would like to go through what a British woman experienced. Because she had already started a course of hepatitis B vaccination when she found she was pregnant, she wanted to know whether or not to continue the course. The local laboratory did a test and found, to everybody's fright, antigens. The doctors concluded that the woman had hepatitis B and that an abortion was inavoidable. Luckily, the woman insisted on repeating the tests in Hong Kong before consenting to the abortion. There it was found that the blood contained only the perfectly harmless antibodies.

CHECKLIST

What to do before going to China

1. See your GP for a general health check-up (take the visa application health certificate form with you, for your doctor to fill in).

2. Have an Aids test and a chest X-ray done (both required for visa application).

3. Have your blood group analysed.

4. Have *all* the vaccinations recommended above.

5. Buy your first aid kit, additional needles, and any medicines you think are necessary.

6. Buy enough multivitamin tablets for the duration of your stay.

7. Take out emergency health insurance (unless your western employer has already done it for you).

What to do on arrival in China

1. Find out where the nearest pharmacies, doctors, dentists and hospitals are.

2. Check how clean the clinics and hospitals appear.

3. Talk to other expatriates about their impressions and experiences of local healthcare. Which doctors, clinics, hospitals do they recommend?

4. Keep your living quarters as clean and hygienic as you possibly can.

5. Buy a stock of frequently needed medicines. You can get good traditional Chinese remedies for sinusitis, common cold and diarrhoea.

6. Exchange information about your blood groups, cases of asthma and allergies with other expats.

CASE STUDIES

At the doctor's

A German woman describes her visit to the doctor: 'I had terrible migraines and a bad cough. The doctor lined nine patients up, asked us to lean over her desk and looked into our mouths. She diagnosed sore throat for each of us, and gave each the same prescription. I persisted, and described my symptoms with the help of gestures. She smiled, asked me to teach her son English, and wrote another prescription. I ended up with 21 different medicines, including a western flu remedy three years past its sell-by date and in five times the recommended dosage, as well as opium, and some white pills which one of my students had had prescribed for asthma and another student to cure a broken leg.

'Antibiotic injections were part of the treatment. I had to bare my bum there and then, in front of others. The men looked discreetly away, but all the females stared at their first ever European bum. The nurse was surprised that I insisted on using my own needles. "We clean our needles very thoroughly after each use," she said, pointing to a rusty tea kettle. I used my friendliest smile and said that as I had the needles, she could just as well help herself to some. She was delighted to increase her stock, and gave me some rice cakes in exchange.'

Hospital

Another patient experienced a hospital in the northeast: 'The doctor who diagnosed pneumonia obviously did not know how to handle the stethoscope. Her once white coat was greasy grey-brown and stained. The nurse who put me on the penicillin drip had black fingernails and greasy hands with which she held the needle before inserting it into the back of my hand. There were about twenty patients in the room, all spitting on the floor. The ground was covered in green, yellow and bloody sputum. Children were peeing on the floor, nobody cleaned up the mess.'

Dentist

A VSO volunteer comments on dental treatment: 'I had to ask the dentist to wash his hands! But apparently, he did a good job, because when I returned to the UK my dentist there said the fillings were made in a very outdated, but solid way, and showed excellent craftsmanship.'

11
Returning Home

SAYING ZAIJIAN

Zaijian means good bye. If you have spent a long time in China, you have probably made good friends, and it is possible that you will never see them again. Start early to exchange addresses and photos.

Spend some time taking photographs of your friends, of your home, the college campus, the town and the rural scenery. Your friends in your home country want to see pictures! If you want to earn money by giving illustrated talks or selling travel articles, you need a selection of slides.

Giving a farewell banquet

Chinese custom demands that the person who is leaving invites friends to a farewell banquet. You may have to give several banquets: one for your colleagues, one for your students, one for your friends . . . so you'd better budget for it in advance!

During the banquet, everyone will say a toast, praising and thanking you. You do the same, praising the Chinese in general and your friends in particular, and say what a wonderful time you've had. If you have a grudge against someone who did his best to make your life hell, this is *not* the occasion to mention it.

Remember to say good bye officially to everyone with whom you had any dealings.

Gifts for your Chinese friends

Your friends will probably buy some gifts for you—which you may not like at all, because they are kitschy (pink porcelain ashtrays printed with gold and orange flowers), because they are too heavy to fit into the tight luggage allowance, and because your friends have spent more than they could afford!

Accept the unwanted gifts with a smile and thanks, and give them to someone else. Better still, tell everyone months in advance that unfortunately you are not allowed to take more with you than a few clothes, and that you will have to leave many things behind. Repeat this on every opportunity. Tell your really close friends that you don't want any gifts. This will at least reduce the number of unwanted presents, especially bulky ones.

Of course, you must have gifts for your friends at hand. Don't buy anything valuable if you have told them that you don't want gifts from them, or they will feel they've lost face. On the other hand, if someone who is not a close friend has done you a substantial favour during your stay, you can reciprocate with a more valuable gift.

The most welcome gifts are those which are 'western', something which you have brought from your home country. Ask your friends at home to send you suitable items a few months before you leave.

The best gifts are:

- Illustrated books with many photos of, for example, English villages or Scottish towns. They can be bought cheaply from bargain book shops.
- Stamps, mint or used, in a small album or a nice envelope.
- Any liqueur or spirit, made in your home country.
- Any foodstuffs (biscuits, sweets, marmalades . . .) made in your home country.

FILLING IN FORMS

Before leaving the country, you are supposed to return your green and orange card to the local authorities. However, you may still need your green card to buy a ticket, or to obtain reduced admission to museums on your way. Hold on to it and give it up to the authorities at the airport if required.

At the airport, you have to fill in an exit card. This is a small white slip of paper, asking for your name, occupation, visa number etc. Supplies of them are lying around on a table at the airport. Have a pen ready.

FINDING SOUVENIRS

Ideas for every budget

Many things which have become part of your daily life in China will add that certain extra to your home—and you cannot buy them outside China, or only at a much higher price. In addition, your friends and family will enjoy typically Chinese gifts.

The cheapest souvenirs are those which don't cost anything at all: used stamps, railway tickets and admission tickets to sights. The latter are indeed very beautiful, real little works of art, if sold at tourist prices. The cheaper ones sold at 'Chinese' prices look somewhat less impressive.

Other very low cost souvenirs are mint stamps, Chinese spices (buy them in plastic sachets in the department store rather than wrapped in paper in the street market). Chinese newspapers and magazines, maps of China (a nice large one is available from the Foreign Language Bookstore in Beijing), tapes with Chinese traditional and folk music, and green jasmine tea.

Available in many different price ranges are fans (paper, silk, feather, sandalwood), silk scarves and ties, embroidered handkerchiefs, cushion covers and wall hangings.

Other items which are much cheaper to buy in China are ginseng (whole roots or prepared slices), silk (a good selection in the number one building of the Beijing Friendship Hotel), silk underwear (small sizes only), tablecloths, those very efficient large thermos flasks, rice bowls and chopsticks.

Jade jewellery is also a popular gift or souvenir for those who can afford it.

SENDING THINGS HOME

If you are returning by air, you will probably have a very limited luggage allowance which doesn't permit you to take all the things you have acquired and cherished during your stay.

Most small post offices will simply refuse to accept parcels abroad. Yes, there are rules, regulations and instructions on how to do it in a book somewhere—but why search for the book and get involved in all sorts of complicated procedures if you can simply send the foreigner home, saying 'mei you' (we don't have it) or 'bu xing' (we can't do that).

Bigger post offices agree to accept parcels, but the prices, conditions and procedures vary. It is only once a year or so that they are requested to perform this duty, so they have to discuss at length the correct formalities. Be prepared to spend three consecutive days at the post office, arguing, negotiating, pleading and form-filling. Don't leave it to the last day when you are in a hurry!

If you are flying from Beijing, you can spend a few days there and post all your parcels from the International Post Office. The staff there are accustomed to sending mail abroad. It will still take a while, because the International Post Office is a large building with many counters, and you may be sent from one counter to another until all requirements are fulfilled.

Even better, you can post your parcels from the small post office at the Friendship Hotel. Staff there are routined at sending mail abroad, and because it's a small post office, they do it themselves and quickly. They will select suitable cardboard boxes, pack your belongings into them and tie them up with string, stick the postage stamp on and postmark them. Don't rely on the rates displayed on the board though: these are out of date, and a board with new rates has not yet been supplied.

If you decide to airmail your belongings, there are two rates: one for ordinary goods, and one for printed matter, which is considerably cheaper. If you have to decide what to take with you on board the airplane, and what to post, it's worth sorting out all books, brochures and maps and posting them.

The people interviewed for this book all confirmed that their belongings arrived safely, five to fourteen days after dispatch.

If you have a lot of goods to send, it is cheaper to send them by sea. Have a crate made—one cubic metre is a useful standard size—fill it tightly and pad it well. If available, add mothballs and desiccants to protect your belongings against rats and seawater, just in case. Delivery can take up to twelve months.

AT BEIJING AIRPORT

As with most airports, Beijing airport requires passengers to arrive at least one and a half hours before departure.

Make sure you have sufficient Chinese cash left to pay for airport tax, use of trolley, any excess luggage, and for drinks or food in case the flight is delayed. If your luggage exceeds the allowance a little, the airport staff may or may not be tolerant. Sometimes they are very strict about the shape and size of your hand luggage rather than the weight. Check the current requirements before you pack your luggage.

There are a couple of bistros at the airport. There is also a money change, which, however, refuses to change surplus Chinese money into foreign currency, except US$. You have little choice but to spend your remaining yuan there and then.

The souvenir stalls are well kept and have a variety of good items on display. These are a good deal more expensive than they would be in other parts of China, and even dearer than in Beijing's tourist spots. However, the selection is good and you still pay far less than you would at home. You can find silk scarves and ties, cushion covers, ginseng, tea, some illustrated books (expensive), chopsticks and paper fans.

Investigate as soon as possible from which gate your flight is leaving. Beijing Airport is not fully equipped with modern electronic information boards, and some travellers find that the signposting is not satisfactory.

Useful Addresses

EMBASSIES, GOVERNMENT OFFICES, AUTHORITIES AND UN ORGANISATIONS

British Embassy, Cultural and Education Section, 4th Floor Landmark Building, 8 North Dongsanhuan Road, Chaoyang District, Beijing 1000026. Tel: (01) 501 1903. Fax: (01) 501 1977.

Chinese Association for the International Exchange of Personnel (CAIEP), Representative Office, 78 Gordon Road, Ealing, London W5 2AR, Tel: (0181) 991 5779. Fax: (0181) 998 5452.

Delegation of Commission of European Communities, Room 2-6-1, Tayuan Diplomatic Office Building, 14 Liangmahe Nan Lu, Beijing 100600. Tel: (01) 532 4443. Fax: (01) 532 4342.

Embassy of the Federal Republic of Germany (German Embassy), 5 Dong Zhi Men Wai Da Jie, Beijing 100600. Tel: (01) 532 2161. Fax: (01) 532 5336. Passport department: Donghua Men Bei Chi Zi 85. Tel: (01) 532 5556.

Embassy of Canada, 19 Dongzhimenwai Dajie, Chaoyangqu, Beijing 100600. Tel: (01) 532 3536. Fax: (01) 532 4072.

Embassy of Ireland, 3 Ritan Dong Lu, Jianguomenwai, 100600. Tel: (01) 532 2691.

Embassy of the Kingdom of the Netherlands, 1-15-2 Tayuan Building for Diplomatic Missions, 14 Liangmahe Nan Lu, Beijing 100600. Tel: (01) 532 1131. Fax: (01) 532 4689.

Embassy of New Zealand, 1 Ritan Donger Jie, Chaoyangqu, Beijing. Tel: (01) 532 27313. Fax: (01) 532 4317.

Embassy of the Republic of Malta, 2-1-22 Tayuangongyu, Beijing. 532 3114.

Embassy of Sweden, 3 Dongzhimenwai Dajie, Sanlitun, Beijing 100600. Tel: (01) 532 3331. Fax: (01) 532 3803.

Embassy of the United States of America, 3 Xiushui Dong Jie, Jianguomenwai, Beijing 100600. Tel: (01) 532 3831.
Embassy of the People's Republic of China, 31 Portland Place, London W1N 3AG, UK. Tel: (0171) 636 1835.
Taipei Representative Office in The UK, 50 Grosvenor Gardens, London SW1W 0EB, UK. Tel: (0171) 396 9151.
United Nations Food and Agriculture Organization (FAO), 4-2-151 Jianguomenwai, Beijing. Tel: (01) 532 28357. Fax: (01) 532 5042.
United Nations Children's Fund (UNICEF), 12 Sanlitun Lu, Beijing 100600. Tel: (01) 532 31318. Fax: (01) 532 3107.
United Nations Population Fund (UNFPA), United Nations Building, 2 Dongqi Jie, Sanlitun, Beijing 100600. Tel: (01) 532 3731. Fax: (01) 532 2567.
World Food Programme (WFP), 2 Dongqi Jie, Sanlitun, Beijing 100600. Tel: (01) 532 3731. Fax: (01) 532 4802.
World Health Organisation (WHO), 9-2-151 Ta Yuan Diplomatic Compound, 1 Xingdong Lu, Dongzhimenwai, Beijing 100600. Tel: (01) 532 5633. Fax: (01) 532 2359.

WESTERN ORGANISATIONS AND COMPANIES WITH A CHINA INTEREST

British Council, Medlock Street, Manchester M15 4AA, UK. Tel: (0161) 957 7000. Fax: (0161) 957 7111.
British Executive Service Overseas (BESO) 164 Vauxhall Bridge Road, London SW1V 2RB, UK. Tel: (0171) 630 066. Fax: (0171) 830 0624.
China-Britain Trade Group, Fifth Floor, Abford House, 15 Wilton Road, London SW1V 1LT, UK. Tel: (0171) 828 5176. Fax: (0171) 630 5780.
The China Business Centre, University Keele, Keele, Staffordshire, ST5 5BG, UK. Tel: (01782) 621111. Fax: (01782) 613847.
China National Tourist Office, 4 Glentworth Street, London NW1, UK. Tel: (0891) 200273.
Chinese Economic Association in the United Kingdom, R432, STICERD, London School of Economics, Houghton Street, London WC2A 2AE, UK. Tel: (0171) 955 6691. Fax: (0171) 242 2357.

Cultural Tours Ltd, 320 Regent Street, London W1R 5AB, UK. Tel: (0171) 636 7906. Fax: (0171) 436 3053.

The Great Britain–China Centre, 15 Belgrave Square, London SW1X 8PS, UK. Tel: (0171) 235 6696. Fax: (0171) 245 6885.

Majestic Trading Co Ltd, 2nd Floor, 70 Piccadilly, London W1V 9HH, UK. Tel: (0171) 629 1516. Fax: (0171) 499 8730.

The Project Trust, The Hebridean Centre, Isle of Coll, Argyll, Scotland, PA78 6TE, UK. Tel: (018793) 444. Fax: (018793) 357.

The Royal Institute of International Affairs, Chatham House, 10 St James's Square, London SW1Y 4LE. Tel: (0171) 957 5700. Fax: (0171) 957 5710.

The Royal Society, China Exchanges, 6 Carlton House Terrace, London SW1Y 5AG. Tel: (0171) 839 5561. Fax: (0171) 930 2170.

Taiwan Trade Centre, 3rd Floor, 29 Wilson Street, London EC2M 2SJ, UK. Tel: (0171) 638 4982. Fax: (0171) 638 4686.

University of London School of Oriental and African Studies, Department of Law and Centre for Chinese Studies, Thornhough Street, Russell Square, London WC1H 0XG, UK. Tel: (0171) 637 2388. Fax: (0171) 436 3844.

Voluntary Services Overseas (VSO), 317 Putney Bridge Road, London SW15 2PN. Tel: (0181) 780 2266. Fax: (0181) 780 1326.

World Expeditions Ltd, 7 North Road, Maidenhead, Berkshire SL6 1PE, UK. Tel: (01628) 74174. Fax: (01628) 74312.

YMCA, International Office for Asia, OSCY, 909-4th Ave, Seattle, Washington 98104, USA. Tel: (0206) 382 5008. Fax: (0206) 382 7283.

ADDRESSES IN THE PEOPLE'S REPUBLIC OF CHINA

ACMR Market Research, 3 Yuetan Beijie, Beijing 2100037. Tel: (01) 861 833 6084 (information consultancy), (01) 861 833 6085 (market research, (01) 861 835 4718 (data services).

Alcanta International School, Rongqui, Shunde, Chuangdong. Tel: (07653) 686338.

American Attorneys, Frederick W Hong, Suite 721, Garden Office Tower, 368 Huanshi Dong Road, Guangzhou, China. Tel: (020) 333 6999 ext 721. Fax: (020) 384 1625.

The Amity Foundation, 17 Da Jian Yin Xiang, Nanjing, China.
Beijing Automobile Repair Co, 72 Youanmennei Dajie, Beijing. Tel: (01) 322531.
Beijing Dongzhimenwai Dairy Product Factory, 40 Dong Zhong Street, Dongzhimenwai, Beijing. Tel: (01) 466 3218.
Beijing Large Goods and Materials Transportation Co, 10 Guangyi Jie, Xuanwuqu, Neijing 100053. Tel: (01) 338 551.
Beijing Materials Storage and Transportation Co, Yangrou Lane, Xisi, Xichenqu, Beijing 100034. Tel: (01) 603 4143.
Beijing Railway Station, Passenger Enquiries. Tel: (01) 554866.
Beijing Review, 24 Baiwanzhuang Road, Beijing 100037.
Beijing Seed Corporation, 15 Beitaipingzhuang, Haidian District, Beijing. Tel: (01) 201 9342.
Beijing University, Haidian District, Beijing. Tel: (01) 282471.
Beijing University of Post and Telecommunications, 213 Xinxiang, Beijing. Tel: (01) 326 0993.
British Broadcasting Corp (BBC) 2-2 Bangonglou, Sanlitun, 100600. Tel: (01) 532 3777. Fax: (01) 532 4691.
Canadian Airlines International, Room 135, Jianguo Hotel, Jiangiomenwai Da Jie, Beijing 100020. Tel: (01) 500 1956/500 3950. Fax: (01) 500 2871.
China Daily, no 15 Hui Xin Dongje, Chaoyang District, Beijing 100029. Tel: (01) 422 4488. Fax: (01) 422 0922.
China Europe Management Institute Shanghai. Jiaotong University, Minhang Campus, 800 Dongchuanlu, Shanghai 200240. Tel: (021) 425 9365. Fax: (021) 435 8928.
China National Tree and Seed Corporation (Gardening Supplies), c/o The Ministry of Forestry, 18 Hepingli Dongjie, Chaoyang District, Beijing. Tel: (01) 421 4717.
China Pictorial Publications, Hua Yuan Cun, Beijing 100044. Fax: (01) 841 3023.
Fangcaodi Primary School, 1 Ritan Beilu, Chaoyangmenwai, Chaoyang District, Beijing. Tel: (01) 509 4328.
Gallup Market Research, G-202, POB 9788, Asian Games Village, Beijing 100101. Tel: (01) 491 1293. Fax: (01) 499 1749.
German School, c/o Lido Hotel, Jiangtailu, Chaoyang District, Beijing. Tel: (01) 436 1953.
Heilongjiang Foreign Trade and Economy Exhibition Centre, 40 Xidazhijie, Harbin City, Heilongjiang Province. Tel: (0451) 363 3756. Fax: (0451) 364 9797.

International School, Jiangtailu, Chaoyang District, Beijing. Tel: (01) 437 6688 ext 1242.

International Study Group, Sanlitun, Block 1, Entrance 3, Apartment 1, Beijing. Tel: (01) 532 2293.

ISS Beijing International School, 17 Area 4, An Zen Xi Li, Chaoyang District, Beijing 100029. Tel: (01) 426 1059, 426 4995.

Lufthansa, German Airlines, Beijing Lufthansa Centre, 50 Liang Ma Quiao Road, Chaoyang District, Beijing 100016. Tel: (01) 465 4488. Fax: (01) 465 3223.

Lufthansa Centre Kindergarten, 50 Liangmahe, Chaoyang District, Beijing. Tel: (01) 465 2021.

National Materials Storage and Transportation Group, 25 Yetan Bei Jie, Beijing 100834. Tel: (01) 839 2543. Fax: (01) 839 2535.

Office Equipment Company, Beijing Kangde Group, Room 101–102, 47 Chongnei Dajie, Chongwen District, Beijing 10005. Tel: (01) 204 2959. Fax: (01) 203 3364.

Pakistan College of Beijing, 1 Sanlitun, Dongzhimenwai, Chaoyang District, Beijing. Tel: (01) 532 1905.

Railway Technical Information Research Institute/China Academy of Railway Sciences, No 2 Daliushu Road, Xizhimenwai Beijing 100081.

Shanghai Star, Rm 204, Hengshan Hotel, 534 Hengshan Rd, Shanghai 200030. Tel: (021) 473 9471. Fax: (021) 433 5306.

Sino-German Policlinic, Landmark Tower, B-1, 8 North Dong San Huan Road, Chao Yang District, Beijing, 100004. Tel: (01) 501 1983. Fax: (01) 501 1944.

ADDRESSES IN THE REPUBLIC OF CHINA

ELSI Taiwan Language School, 12 Kuling Street, Taipei. Tel: (02) 321 9005.

Hess Language School, Po Ai Road, No83 2F, Taipei. Tel: (02) 383 5440. Fax: (02) 382 0799.

Tourism Bureau, 9/F1, 280 Chunghsiao E. Rd, Sec. 4, PO Box 1490, Taipei. Tel: (02) 721 8541. Fax: (02) 773 5487.

Further Reading

BOOKS

Barefoot in the Boardroom—Venture and Misadventure in the People's Republic of China, by Bill Purves. Allen & Unwin, Sydney, Australia. Written in an entertaining and informative style, giving facts, observations, first-hand experiences and advice for businesspeople.

China on Business, The Economist Publications. A well structured, user-friendly book which is lightweight, so it won't cause any problems with your luggage allowance.

China to 2000—Reform's Last Chance, by Simon Long. *The Economist* Intelligence Unit. Historical and economical overview with plenty of statistics.

A Business Guide to China, by Ron Breth and Jin Kaiping. Victoria College Press, USA 1988. The book is informative but does not exactly make easy, entertaining reading, as the language is somewhat heavy, weighed down with bureaucracy. Useful for those who mean serious business.

Simple Etiquette in China, by Caroline Mason. Paul Norbury Publications, 1989. A small handbook, arranged in practical subjects such as *Hotels and Living Conditions, Presents and Shopping, Conversation and Communications*. Information is given in brief paragraphs. The book is lightweight and user-friendly, recommended for reading and reference. The money section is out of date.

Study Chinese in China. Compiled by the Chinese Society for Teaching Chinese as a Foreign Language. Published by Beijing Language & Culture University Press. Contains profiles and addresses of universities, language institutes and so on. Written in public relations style, praising everything Chinese as 'excellent'. Very informative.

The Foreign Expert's Handbook—A Guide to Living & Working in China, compiled by the State Bureau of Foreign Experts. Published by China International Book Trading Corporation, Beijing, 1988. A useful book to have, although the language is somewhat bureaucratic, and much of the contents are obvious—for example 'Smoking in bed should be carefully watched in case of fire'. Sometimes, the book is a little evasive on subjects where the reader would require facts, and it describes certain aspects of Chinese life in too glowing terms. Not everyone would, for example, agree with the statement 'China is one of the safest countries in the world, although of course the elimination of crime is a long process, and for foreigners there are few problems in this respect'.

Doing Business with China edited by Jonathan Reuvid. Published by Kogen Page, 1994. 560 pages, £75.00. Probably the most up-to-date guide to the Chinese market, this book contains surveys of industry and business practice and statistical data. One of its strengths is its analysis of China's 46 prime business locations.

Travellers Health, edited by Dr Richard Dawood. Published by Oxford University Press. Paperback, 472 pages. This book has been written with adventurous tourists as well as expats in mind. Although it has no chapter specifically about China, it gives a lot of advice on how to cope with the climate, how to stay healthy in difficult circumstances, and how to diagnose and treat ailments.

The Directory of British Organisations with a China Interest. Published by the Great Britain—China Centre. 134 pages in ring binder format. This book gives hundreds of address of relevant organisations, complete with addresses, aims, activities and so on. Regularly updated; good index. Indispensible for further research.

Culture Shock! China, by Kevin Sinclair and Iris Wong Po- yee. Published by Kuperard. Paperback, 270 pages. Probably the best book to prepare you for the Chinese culture and mentality, written in a highly entertaining style. However, it has been written mostly with the wealthy western businessman in mind, and includes advice such as how to deal with domestic servants which may be of limited value to the average English teacher in China.

A Brief Introduction to The Republic of China, published by the

Taiwan Government Information Office. Paperback, 219 pages. A lot of information in compact format, covering everything from government and law to education, from foreign relations to housing and accommodation.

Wild Swans by Jung Chang. Published by HarperCollins/Flamingo. Paperback, 696 pages, £7.99. This brilliantly written book covers the lives of three generations of Chinese women: the author's grandmother (concubine of a warlord), her mother (officer in the red army) and herself (worker and university student). Most of the expats interviewed for *Living and Working in China* agreed that *Wild Swans* taught them more about Chinese history, and the effect of historical events on people, than the best history or reference book ever could.

Living in China by Rebecca Weiner, Margaret Murphy and Albert Li. Published by China Books & Periodicals. Targeted mostly at English teachers who plan to work in the Republic of China or the People's Republic of China, this book gives valuable advice. It also contains a list of Chinese colleges and universities which employ foreign teachers, complete with addresses and comments from those who've worked there. Clearly written with American readers in mind, it is still useful for other nationals. Some information (eg on prices and currencies) is outdated. Available by mail order from China Books, Box S, 2929 Twenty-fourth Street, San Francisco, CA 94110, USA. Tel: (415) 282 2994. Fax: (415) 282 0994. Write for current price and air/sea mail rates.

English Teaching Handbook for China, compiled by VSO Field Office in Beijing. The perfect source of information for everything you will ever want to know about teaching English in China. Contains contributions by experienced teachers. Not available in bookshops. Try obtaining a copy in exchange for a donation to VSO funds, or borrow one from a returned volunteer. There is also a copy in the library of the Great Britain–China Centre, which you can read, and if you are a member, you are entitled to borrow it.

China Bound Revised, by Anne Thurston. Published by National Academy Press in Washington. Although the contents are slanted mostly at American readers, this book offers a lot of practical advice. Recently updated.

China: A Travel Survival Guide, by Alan Samagalski. Published by Lonely Planet. Most of the foreigners in China who were interviewed for *Living and Working in China* declared this book to be their favourite travel guide. Particularly useful for budget travel.

PERIODICALS

China–Great Britain Trade Review. Monthly journal of the China–Britain Trade Group, free to members.

Britain–China. Magazine of the Great Britain–China Centre, published three times a year, free to members.

Overseas Jobs Express. Newspaper for jobhunters worldwide. Twenty-four issues per year. Often with features about China and job vacancies. Available by subscription. Address: PO Box 22, Brighton, BN1 6HX, UK.

Jobs International. A recently launches monthly magazine on working abroad. Address: Cromwell Court, New Road, St Ives, Cambs PE17 4BG, UK.

China Daily. Chinese daily newspaper in English language. Very well written and informative, sometimes critical, but takes government view on sensitive subjects. Nicknamed 'The Good News' by expatriates for its tendency to always give at least one positive aspect to all home news (not to foreign news, though). No 15 Hui Xin Dongje, Chaoyang District, Beijing 100029. Tel: (01) 422 4488. Fax: (01) 422 0922.

China Pictorial. Large glossy magazine of cultural and tourist interest, published monthly in Chinese, Tibetan, Korean, Russian, English, German, French, Japanese, Hindi, Spanish, Arabic, Swahili, Italian, Urdu and Thai. China Pictorial Publications, Hua Yan Cun, Beijing 100044. Fax: (01) 841 3023.

Beijing Weekend. Published every Friday in Beijing. No 15 Jui Xin Dongje, Chaoyang District, Beijing 100029. Tel: (01) 422 0332. Fax: (01) 422 0922.

Shanghai Star. Published every Tuesday and Friday in Shanghai, in English language. Contents most relevant to Shanghai area, but read nationwide. Tabloid format. Rm 204, Hengshan Hotel, 534 Hengshan Rd, Shanghai 200030. Tel: (021) 473 9471. Fax: (021) 433 5306.

Beijing Reciew. 24 Baiwanzhuang Road, Beijing 100037. Weekly magazine, published on Mondays. The title is misleading, as it covers all China. Excellent features and some news articles.

Although it sticks strictly to the Chinese government viewpoint on sensitive subjects, it can be surprisingly frank and is highly informative. Also available outside China by subscription.

Survival Chinese (Mandarin) & Glossary

bread	mianbao
classmate	tongxue
envelope	xinfeng
good	hao
good bye	zaijian
head of department	zhuren
hello	ni hao
how much is it?	duoshao qian?
how old are you?	ni duo da le?
I am . . . American	Wo she . . . Meiguo ren
. . . British	. . . Yinguo ren
. . . Canadian	. . . Jianada ren
. . . Chinese	. . . Zhongguo ren
. . . Dutch	. . . Halan ren
. . . German	. . . Deguo ren
. . . Irish	. . . Aijilan
I don't eat meat	wo bu chi rou
I want . . .	wo yao . . .
I want this	wo yao zheige
I want one of this	wo yao yi ge zheige
I want two pounds	wo yao liang jin
married/unmarried	jiehun/meiyou jiehun
no thanks	bu xiexie
parents	fumu
please come in	quing jin
please drink tea	qing he cha
postage stamp	youpiao
post office	youju
railway station	huochezhan
rice (cooked)	mifan
student	xuesheng

telephone	dianhua
thank you	xiexie
teacher	laoshi
(gents/ladies) toilet	(nan/nü) cesuo
too expensive	tai gui le
tomatoes	xihongshi
vegetables	shucai
where is . . . ?	. . . zai nar?
worker	gongren

Numbers

1	yi	6	liu
2	er (or liang)	7	qi
3	san	8	ba
4	si	9	jiu
5	wu	10	shi

GLOSSARY

waiban the foreign teacher's contact at the foreign affairs office.

putonghua the official Chinese language, spoken in most parts of China (also called Mandarin or Han Chinese)

pinyin the 'new' way of writing Chinese in Latin alphabet, now commonly used on mainland China, but not always understood by older people and in rural areas

PRC People's Republic of China, also called mainland China or communist China

ROC Republic of China, also called Taiwan

renminbi the currency in the People's Republic of China

Index